Humanism and Terror

Humanism and Terror

An Essay on the
Communist Problem
by Maurice Merleau-Ponty
Translated and with Notes
by John O'Neill

BEACON PRESS : BOSTON

First published in French as *Humanisme et Terreur,*
Essai sur le Problème Communiste © 1947, Éditions Gallimard

English translation copyright © 1969 by Beacon Press

Library of Congress catalog card number: 71–84796

Beacon Press books are published under the auspices
of the Unitarian Universalist Association

Printed in the United States of America

International Standard Book Number: 0–8070–0277–1
Second printing, September 1971

Contents

v

157467

Translator's Note

Humanism and Terror first appeared in 1947. It is the translator's belief that Merleau-Ponty's argument, as well as that of Koestler in *Darkness at Noon* (1946) raises questions that are still relevant to the fateful connection between revolution and violence. All the same, it may be useful to contemporary readers to recall some of the background to the dispute between Koestler and Merleau-Ponty and the way it involved intellectuals on the French left whether Communist or non-Communist.

I shall not attempt to trace in any detail the postwar developments which are the setting for *Humanism and Terror*. To do this would involve a knowledge of the history of the French Communist Party and the spectrum of French socialism or left thought which is beyond the translator's competence. Fortunately, there are a number of such studies to which the reader may be referred.[1]

[1] David Caute, *Communism and the French Intellectuals,* New York, The Macmillan Company, 1964, has an excellent bibliography; Charles A. Micaud, *Communism and the French Left,* London, Weidenfeld and Nicolson, 1963; Alfred J. Rieber, *Stalin and the French Communist Party,* New York and London,

Merleau-Ponty's argument is especially difficult to understand if the radical alternatives forced upon French politics
by the Cold War split between America and the Soviet
Union is accepted without question. In 1947 there was still
a chance, at least in the mind of a non-Communist left
intellectual like Merleau-Ponty, that France and Europe
would not have to become a satellite either to America or
the Soviet Union. The hopes of the Resistance for immediate revolutionary change after the war had withered away
in the tripartist tangles of the Communists, Socialists, and
Christian Democrats. In March 1947, the Truman doctrine
was initiated and in April the Big Four discussions on Germany failed. The introduction of the Marshall Plan in June
of the same year, condemned by Molotov's walkout on the
Paris Conference in July, hastened the breakdown of tripartism. Suspicion of the anti-Soviet implications of the
Marshall Plan caused many of the Left to look toward a
neutralist position for Europe, but made them uncertain
whether to build this position around the Socialist Party,
which had failed so far to take any independent line, or the
Communist Party, which could be expected to follow a
Soviet line. But the drift was toward a pro-Western, anti-
Soviet European integration led by the center and right
elements of the French Third Force, including the Gaullists.
Within two years, the formation of the Brussels Treaty Organization, the North Atlantic Treaty Organization, and

Columbia University Press, 1962; George Lichtheim, *Marxism in Modern France,*
New York and London, Columbia University Press, 1966; Frederick F. Ritsch,
The French Left and the European Idea, 1947–1949, New York, Pageant Press,
1966; B. D. Graham, *The French Socialists and Tripartisme, 1944–1947,* Toronto,
The University of Toronto Press, 1965.

the Soviet Cominform brought down the iron curtain of which Winston Churchill had spoken in his Fulton Speech in March of 1946.

The intellectual French Left was in an impossible situation which no combination of Marxism or existentialism seemed capable of remedying. French capitalism was bad, but American capitalism was even more anathema to the left, if only because it was in the rudest of health internationally, though perhaps not at home. At the same time, French socialism was anything but independent and its chances looked no better with Communist help. In such a situation it was impossible to be an anti-Communist if this meant being pro-American, witnessing the Americanization of Europe, and foreswearing the Communists who had fought bravely in the Resistance. On the other hand, it was not possible to be a Communist if this meant being blind to the hardening of the Soviet regime and becoming a witness to the Communist brand of imperialism which broke so many Marxist minds.

It is not surprising that many on the Left as well as the Right were unable to bear such ambiguity and therefore welcomed any sign to show clearly which side to support, even if it meant a "conversion" to the most extreme left and right positions. The attention drawn to those whose god had failed them is thus understandable.[2]

Koestler's *Darkness at Noon* reveals in its very title the gift of antithesis which generates a bad conversion for the lack of a genuine synthesis, which might have been achieved if Koestler had known how to grasp the lived relation be-

[2] *The God That Failed,* edited by Richard Crossman, New York, Harper, 1949.

tween the senses and ideology in a man's character. This is
not the place to engage in a criticism of the literary qualities of Koestler's novel. It certainly has its truly great moments. But ultimately it fails to come to grips with its
central problem: to create characters who inhabit their own
history and live through choices within it rather than to
present characters who operate by means of simplistic moral
alternatives, decided upon before their story begins.[3] In any
case, Merleau-Ponty's criticism of *Darkness at Noon* eschews
its literary qualities, even though these are not independent
of its political and moral logic, which is the focus of
Merleau-Ponty's own essay.

The nature of the relation between communism and the
French intellectuals has not been exhausted by any of the
political, psychological, or sociological studies which have
tackled it. *Darkness at Noon* may have killed communism
for many people, but it also produced converts. But the issue
that concerned Merleau-Ponty was not the life of communism as an institution. He was well aware of the changes in
Communist institutions. He understood that the Revolution
was learning to live with history. What he wanted to get at
was how it had happened that theoretical Marxism had
hardened into the dogma that made the views on history
and politics of Koestler's Commissar a plausible account of
Marxism. Insofar as Soviet communism was represented in
Koestler's portrait and in the revelations that came with the

[3] John O'Neill, "Situation and Temporality," *Philosophy and Phenomeno-
logical Research,* Vol. XXVIII, No. 3, March 1968, pp. 413–422; Irving Howe,
Politics and the Novel, Cleveland and New York, The World Publishing Company, 1957.

Cominform campaign against Tito, the Rajk-Kosov trials, and the Soviet labor camps, Merleau-Ponty was also a witness to the disenchantment of European Communists. Yet at the same time in *Humanism and Terror* he is engaged in the creative interpretation of theoretical Marxism which was taking hold in France just when communism was beginning to lose its grip on the intellectuals.

Thus, as George Lichtheim points out in his study *Marxism in Modern France,* unless we are able to keep these two developments clear, we shall run the risk of confusing Merleau-Ponty's elaboration of Marxist philosophy of history and revolution with an apologia for the Soviet Union and the Moscow Trials. This is the error made by the hardline French Communists who attacked Merleau-Ponty, failing to see that what they regarded as an anti-Communist argument was simply the destruction of their obsolete Marxist dogmas in a creative interpretation of the kind of Marxist thought that might live in history without the need to be protected from it.[4]

Toronto, Spring 1969

---

[4] John O'Neill, "Revolution and Responsibility," Symposium: Phenomenology and Historical Understanding, Conference on the Philosophy of History and the Social Sciences, York University, Toronto, April 10–12, 1969.

Author's Preface

COMMUNISM is often discussed in terms of the contrast between deception, cunning, violence, propaganda, and the respect for truth, law, and individual consciousness—in short, the opposition between political realism and liberal values. Communists reply that in democracies cunning, violence, propaganda, and *realpolitik* in the guise of liberal principles are the substance of foreign or colonial politics and even of domestic politics. Respect for law and liberty has served to justify police suppression of strikes in America; today[1] it serves even to justify military suppression in Indochina or in Palestine and the development of an American empire in the Middle East. The material and moral culture of England presupposes the exploitation of the colonies. The purity of principles not only tolerates but even requires violence. Thus there is a mystification in liberalism. Judging from history and by everyday events, liberal ideas belong to a system of violence of which, as Marx said, they are the "spiritual *point*

[1] 1947 (Translator).

d'honneur," the "solemn complement" and the "general basis of consolation and justification."[2]

It is a powerful argument. In refusing to judge liberalism in terms of the ideas it espouses and inscribes in constitutions and in demanding that these ideas be compared with the prevailing relations between men in a liberal state, Marx is not simply speaking in the name of a debatable materialist philosophy—he is providing a formula for the concrete study of society which cannot be refuted by idealist arguments. Whatever one's philosophical or even theological position, a society is not the temple of value-idols that figure on the front of its monuments or in its constitutional scrolls; the value of a society is the value it places upon man's relation to man. It is not just a question of knowing what the liberals have in mind but what in reality is done by the liberal state within and beyond its frontiers. Where it is clear that the purity of principles is not put into practice, it merits condemnation rather than absolution. To understand and judge a society, one has to penetrate its basic structure to the human bond upon which it is built; this undoubtedly depends upon legal relations, but also upon forms of labor, ways of loving, living, and dying. The theologian will observe that human relations have a religious significance and are under God's eye. But he will not refuse to adopt them as a touchstone and, on pain of degrading religion to a daydream, he is ultimately obliged to admit that principles and the inner life are alibis the moment they cease to animate external and everyday life. A regime which is nominally liberal can be oppressive in reality. A regime which acknowledges its violence *might* have in it more genuine humanity. To counter Marxism on this with "ethical arguments" is to ignore what Marxism has said with most truth and what has made its fortune in the world; it is to continue a mystification and to bypass the problem. Any serious discussion of communism must therefore pose the problem in communist terms, that is to say, not on the ground of principles but on the ground of human relations. It will not brandish liberal principles in order to topple communism; it will examine whether it is doing anything to resolve the problem rightly raised by communism, namely, to establish among men relations that are human.

This is the spirit in which we have reopened the question of Communist violence which Koestler brought to light in *Darkness at Noon*. We have not examined whether in fact Bukharin led an organized opposition nor whether the execution of the old Bolsheviks was really indispensable to the order and the national defense of the U.S.S.R. We did not undertake to re-enact the 1937 trials. Our purpose was to understand Bukharin as Koestler sought to understand Rubashov. For the trial of Bukharin brings to light the theory and practice of violence under communism since Bukharin exercises violence upon himself and brings about his own condemnation. So we tried to rediscover what he really thought beneath the conventions of language. Koestler's account appeared to us inadequate. Rubashov is in the opposition because he does not support the Party's new policy or its inhuman discipline. But inasmuch as this involves an ethical revolt and his ethics have always been to obey the Party he ends by capitulating unconditionally. Bukharin's "defense" at the Trials goes quite beyond the alternatives of ethics or discipline. From start to finish, Bukharin remains somebody; he may not acknowledge the point of personal honor but he defends his revolutionary honor and rejects the imputation of espionage and sabotage. When he does capitulate, it is therefore not only from discipline. It is because he recognizes in his political conduct, however justified it may once have been, an inevitable ambiguity through which it risks condemnation. In extreme situations, where the whole revolution is questioned, the revolutionary who rallies in opposition surrounds himself with his enemies and can endanger the revolution. Siding with the kulaks against forced collectivization amounts to "imputing to the proletariat the costs of the class struggle." It is threatening the work of the Revolution if the regime becomes wholly caught up in forced collectivization because it has only a limited time in which to bring order into its conflicts. The threat of war changes the significance of opposition. Obviously "treason" is only a political divergence. But divergences in a period of crisis compromise and betray the gains of October 1917.

Those who become indignant at the mere expression of these ideas and refuse to examine them forget that Bukharin paid dearly for the right to be heard and not treated as a scoundrel. For our part, we are trying to understand him— quite apart from trying to establish that he was in the right —and to do this we are turning to our recent experience. For we too have lived through one of those moments where

history is suspended and institutions that are threatened with
extinction demand fundamental decisions from men where
the risk is total because their final outcome depends upon a
conjuncture not entirely foreseeable. When the collaborator
made his decision in 1940 in terms of what he believed to be
the inevitable future (we assume he was disinterested) he
conflicted with those who did not believe in this future nor
want it and thereafter between them and him it was a
matter of force. When one is living in what Péguy called an
historical *period,* in which political man is content to ad-
minister a regime or an established law, one can hope for a
history without violence. When one has the misfortune or
the luck to live in an *epoch,* or one of those moments where
the traditional ground of a nation or society crumbles and
where, for better or worse, man himself must reconstruct
human relations, then the liberty of each man is a mortal
threat to the others and violence reappears.

What we have said is that all discussion from a liberal
perspective misses the problem since it professes to be relevant to a country which has made and intends to continue a
revolution whereas liberalism excludes the revolutionary
hypothesis. One may prefer "periods" to "epochs," one may
think that revolutionary violence does not succeed in transforming human relations—if one wants to understand the
Communist problem, it is necessary to start by placing the
Moscow Trials in the revolutionary *Stimmung*[3] of violence
apart from which they are inconceivable. *Only then does
the discussion begin.* It does not consist in looking to see if
communism respects the rules of liberal thought—it is too

[3] *Stimmung,* style, framework, atmosphere (Translator).

evident that it does not—but in asking whether the violence it exercises is revolutionary and capable of creating human relations between men. The Marxist critique of liberal ideas is so powerful that if communism were on the way to create by world revolution a classless society in which the causes of war and decadence had disappeared, along with the exploitation of man by man, then one would have to be a Communist. But is it on this path? Does the violence in today's communism have the same sense it had in Lenin's day? Is communism still equal to its humanist intentions? That is the real question.

Its intentions are beyond question. Marx draws a radical distinction between human and animal life inasmuch as man creates his means of life, culture, history, and thus evinces a capacity for initiative which is his absolute originality. Marxism looks toward the horizon of the future in which "man is the supreme being for man." The reason Marx does not adopt this intuition of man as the first principle of political action is that in advocating nonviolence one reinforces established violence, or a system of production which makes misery and war inevitable. At the same time, in the return to the play of violence there is the risk of permanent involvement. Thus the essential task of Marxism is to find a violence which recedes with the approach of man's future. This is what Marx believed he had found in proletarian violence, namely, the power of that class of men who, because they are expropriated in present society from their country, their labor, and their very life, are capable of recognizing one another aside from all differences, and thus of founding humanity. Cunning, deception, bloodshed, and dictatorship are justified if they bring the proletariat into power and to that extent alone.

Marxist politics is formally dictatorial and totalitarian. But it is a dictatorship of men who are men first and foremost and a totalitarianism of workers of all kinds who repossess the State and the means of production. The dictatorship of the proletariat is not the will of a few officials who are the only ones initiated in the secret of history, as in Hegel; it follows the spontaneous movement of the proletariat in every country and relies upon the "instinct" of the masses. Lenin may well have insisted upon the authority of the Party to guide the proletariat, who would otherwise, as he says, remain syndicalist and not move on to political action. He nevertheless grants much to the instinct of the masses, at least once the capitalist machine has been smashed, and at the beginning of the Revolution he even goes so far as to say: "There is not nor can there be a concrete plan for the organization of economic life. No one knows how to issue it. Only the masses are capable of that, thanks to their experience . . ." Since he subscribes to class action, the Leninist abandons universal ethics; but he will have it restored in the new universe of the world proletariat. Not just any means is good for the realization of this universe and, for example, there can be no question of systematically deceiving the proletariat and hiding the real issue for very long; in principle that is out because it would diminish class consciousness and compromise the victory of the proletariat. The proletariat and class consciousness are fundamental to the character of Marxist politics; they can to some extent be put in the background if circumstances demand it, but too long or too extensive a shift of this kind would destroy its character. Marx is hostile to the liberal posture of nonviolence, but the violence which he prescribes is not indiscriminate.

Can we say the same of today's communism? In the last ten years in the U.S.S.R. the social hierarchy has become considerably accentuated. The proletariat plays an insignificant role in the Party Congresses. Perhaps political discussion goes on in the cells but it never appears publicly. National Communist parties struggle for power without a proletarian platform and without always avoiding chauvinism. Political differences which previously did not involve the death penalty are not only punished as crimes but are even dressed up as crimes against common law. Terror no longer seeks to advance itself as revolutionary Terror. In the cultural order the dialectic is effectively replaced by the scientific rationalism of the last generation apparently because the dialectic leaves too great a margin for ambiguity and too much scope for divergences. There is an increasing difference between what Communists think and what they write because there is a widening gap between their intentions and their deeds. A Communist who declared himself warmly in agreement with us, having read the first part of this essay, three days later wrote that it is an example of what might be called a solitary vice of the mind, and that we were playing the game of French neo-Fascism. If one tries to evaluate the general orientation of the Communist system, it would be difficult to maintain that it is moving toward the recognition of man by man, internationalism, or the withering away of the State and the realization of proletarian power. Communist behavior has not changed: it is still the same attitude of conflict, the same warlike cunning, the same methodical wickedness, the same distrust, but underwritten less and less by class spirit and revolutionary brotherhood, relying less and less upon the spontaneous convergence of proletarian movements and the truth of its own historical perspective; communism is increasingly strained, more and more it shows its dark side. There is still the same absolute devotion, the same fidelity, and when the need arises, the same heroism. But this selfless gift, these virtues which appeared in all their purity during the war and have since been the unforgettable grandeur of communism are less visible in peacetime because the defense of the U.S.S.R. now demands a cunning politics. All the facts, varying in significance from the scale of salaries in the U.S.S.R. to the double truth of a Parisian journalist, are signs of a growing tension between intentions and action, between behavior and the thought behind it. The Communist has launched the conscience and values of private man in a public undertaking which should return them a hundredfold. He is still waiting for the returns.

Thus we find ourselves in an inextricable situation. The Marxist critique of capitalism is still valid and it is clear that anti-Sovietism today resembles the brutality, hybris, vertigo, and anguish that already found expression in fascism. On the other side, the Revolution has come to a halt: it maintains and aggravates the dictatorial apparatus while renouncing the revolutionary liberty of the proletariat in the Soviets and its Party and abandoning the humane control of the state. It is impossible to be an anti-Communist and it is not possible to be a Communist.

Trotsky only *appears* to break through the deadlock in political reflection. He certainly was aware of the profound change in the U.S.S.R. But he defined it as a counterrevolution and from this concluded that it was necessary to start the 1917 movement over again. The term "counterrevolution" only has a definite meaning if there exists at present in the U.S.S.R. the possibility of an ongoing revolution. But Trotsky himself often described the revolutionary ebb as an unavoidable phenomenon after the failure of the German revolution. To speak of capitulation is to imply that Stalin lacked courage in the face of a situation intrinsically as clear as that of combat.

Now, the ebbing of revolution is by definition a confused period in which the major lines of history are uncertain. In short, Trotsky is schematizing. The Revolution at the time he created it was less clear than when he wrote its history. The permissible limits of violence were not so clearly drawn and it was not always exercised only against the bourgeoisie. In a recent pamphlet, *The Tragedy of the Soviet Writers,* Victor Serge recalls truthfully that Gorki "who maintained a courageous moral independence" and "did not restrict himself to criticism of revolutionary power . . . ended by receiving from Lenin a friendly invitation to exile himself abroad." It is a long way from a friendly invitation to deportation but not a world of difference and Trotsky often forgets it. Just as the Revolution was not as pure as he says, the "counter-revolution" is not so impure and, if we want to judge it without being precious, we should remember that in a country like France it carries with it the greatest part of popular hope. Thus it is not easy to render the diagnosis. Nor is it easy to find a remedy. Since the ebb of revolution has been a world phenomenon, and as a result of diversion and compromise the world proletariat now feels itself even less united, it is a hopeless undertaking to take up the 1917 movement once more.

In sum we can neither begin 1917 over, nor believe that communism can be what it used to want to be, nor consequently hope that in exchange for the "formal" liberties of democracy it will offer us the concrete liberty of a proletarian civilization—without unemployment, without exploitation, and without war. The Marxist transition from formal liberty to actual liberty has not occurred and in the immediate future has no such chance. Marx, however, did not mean to "suppress" liberty, discussion, philosophy, and in general the values of individual conscience except by "realizing" them in the life of everyone. Now that this outcome has become problematic, it is imperative to maintain the habit of discussion, criticism, research, and the apparatus of social and political culture. We must preserve liberty while waiting for a fresh historical impulse which may allow us to engage it in a popular movement without ambiguity. However, the practice and even the idea of liberty can now no longer be what they were before Marx. The right to defend the values of liberty and conscience is ours only if we are sure in doing so that we do not serve the interests of imperialism or become associated with its mystifications. And how shall we be sure of it? By not ceasing to explicate the liberal mystification wherever it rises—in Palestine, in Indochina, and even in France

—by criticizing the liberty-idol on a flag or in a constitution which legitimates the classical means of police and military oppression—and this is the name of a practical freedom which spreads through the lives of everyone, from the Vietnamese or Palestinian peasant to the Western intellectual. We must remember that liberty becomes a false ensign—a "solemn complement" of violence—as soon as it becomes only an idea and we begin to defend liberty instead of free men. It is then claimed that humanity is being preserved despite the miseries of politics; in reality, and at this very moment, one is endorsing a limited politics. It is the essence of liberty to exist only in the practice of liberty, in the inevitably imperfect movement which joins us to others, to the things of the world, to our jobs, mixed with the hazards of our situation. In isolation, or understood as a principle of discrimination, like the law according to St. Paul, liberty is nothing more than a cruel god demanding his hecatombs. An aggressive liberalism exists which is a dogma and already an ideology of war. It can be recognized by its love of the empyrean of principles, its failure ever to mention the geographical and historical circumstances to which it owes its birth, and its abstract judgments of political systems without regard for the specific conditions under which they develop. Its nature is violent, nor does it hesitate to impose itself through violence in accordance with the old theory of the secular arm. There is a way of discussing communism in the name of liberty which consists in mentally suppressing the problems of the U.S.S.R. and which, as the psychoanalysts would say, is a sort of symbolic destruction of the U.S.S.R. In contrast, true liberty takes others as they are,

tries to understand even those doctrines which are its negation, and never allows itself to judge before understanding.[4]
We must fulfill our freedom of thought in the freedom of
understanding. But how are we to transfer this outlook into
daily politics?

The concrete liberty of which we are speaking could have
formed the platform of French communism since World
War II. In principle it is its platform. Since 1941, the official
line of Soviet politics has been in agreement with the Western democracies. Nevertheless, in France the Communists
have not always played the democratic game openly. They
have gone so far as to vote against a government in which
they were represented, and even to get their ministers to
vote against it; and they have been unwilling to commit
themselves to the policy of union, to which they subscribed.
This is, first of all, because they wished to preserve their
prestige as a revolutionary party and, secondly, because,
under the cover of agreement with former allies, they anticipated conflict and before meeting it they wanted to win
solid positions in the state; and, finally, because they have
retained, if not proletarian politics, at least the Bolshevik
style and strictly do not understand what union means.

It is difficult to evaluate the relative weight of these three

---

[4] This is the method that we have followed in this essay. As will be seen,
we have not invoked any other principles against violence than its own. The
same reasons that make it understandable that men are killed in defense of a
revolution (or that one rightly kills in defense of a nation) prevent us from
acknowledging that no one dares kill men except on the pretext of espionage.
The same reasons which make it understandable that the Communists consider
a man who leaves them a traitor prevent us from agreeing that they should hide
it behind police action. When the revolution disguises its opponents it foreswears
its own audacity and its own hope.

motives. Very likely, the first was not decisive, since the Communists have never been seriously threatened on their left. The second must have weighed in their calculations, but one wonders whether they were right. It is beyond doubt that their attitude facilitated a joint movement of the other parties who, being more inclined to liberalism and less well armed for a death struggle, professed respect for "parliamentary loyalty" and reproached the Communists with their lack of it. Of course, had this argument been lacking, anti-Sovietism would have found others to demand the expulsion of the Communists. But they would have had difficulty in achieving this had the Communists openly espoused pluralism, had they committed themselves to the practice and defense of democracy, and had they been able to present themselves as its appointed defenders. Finally, perhaps the Communists would have found more solid guarantees against a Western coalition in the real exercise of democracy than in their attempts to scuttle power. This is more likely since these tactics had at the same time to be cautious and they were in any case unwilling to commit themselves wholly to an aggressive politics.

In the opposition's policy of support without rupture, governmental opposition without dismissal, and now even local strikes without a general strike,[5] we are unable to see, as some do, such a well-directed plan, but rather an oscillation between two kinds of politics which the Communists practice simultaneously without being able to develop either one

[5] We are not saying that the Communists instigate strikes: it is enough, for them to occur, that they are not opposed by the Communists.

fully.[6] Part of this hesitation must be recognized as due to the Bolshevik habituation to violence which makes the Communists seemingly incapable of political union. They cannot conceive of union except with those who are weak enough for them to dominate, just as they only agree to dialogue with mutes. In the cultural order, for example, they force non-Communist writers into the alternative of being adversaries or, as they are called, "useful innocents." The intellectuals whom they prefer are those who never write a word of politics or philosophy and get themselves stuck in the digest of Communist newspapers. As for the others, whenever their writings are received, it is not only with reservations, which would be natural, but also with disobliging moral appreciations, as though to initiate them in one step into the role they deserve—that of martyrs without faith. Communist intellectuals are so unaccustomed to dialogue that they refuse to collaborate in any collective enterprise over which they do not have direct or indirect control. This timidity and underestimation of inquiry is a function of the profound change in contemporary communism, which has ceased to be a confident interpretation of spontaneous history in order to rest upon the defense of the U.S.S.R. Thus, just when they are really giving up the class struggle, the Communists continue to conceive of politics in terms of war, and this compromises their activity in the

6 This equivocation was visible at the *Rencontres Internationales* in Geneva, September 1946, in G. Lukacs' speech, which began with the classical critique of formal democracy and finished by inviting Western intellectuals to re-establish the very democratic ideas that he had just shown to be dead.

liberal field. By trying to win on the proletarian front *and* on the liberal front, it is possible that they will lose on both. It is up to them to know whether it is absolutely necessary to change everyone who is not a Communist into an enemy. To arrive at a genuine politics of union they still have to understand one small fact: not everyone is a Communist and while there are many poor reasons for not being one, there are some which are not dishonorable.

Can we expect that the Communists and the non-Communist left will unite? That would seem naive, though they undoubtedly might come to it through the force of events. The Communists would not want to push their opposition to the point where government became impossible and thus helped the cause of Gaullism. The Socialists would not be able to govern long in the midst of strikes; they are agreed at the moment that a government without the Communists is far from resolving all problems—or, more exactly, that there is no government without the Communists, since if they are not present in it in the form of a ministerial opposition, they turn up outside in the shape of a proletarian opposition.

Today the formation of governments can only be understood from the perspective of the next war, and unless there is a war today's adversaries will have to collaborate again. This would have to be to some good. For that reason one can only deplore contemporary events. It was possible to understand how one Sunday Léon Blum solemnly rose to speak, formulating the conditions of a union government, demanding that the Communists assume their full responsibilities in it and commit themselves once and for all. But,

in furtively replacing the Communist ministers the Socialists have in turn switched from political action to manipu-
lation. By resorting to the financial establishment in order
to solve their immediate problems, or resuming a colonialist
position on the problem of Indochina, they leave their opponents, whose politics are no less timid, the easy advantage
of presenting themselves as the only "progressive" party.
Thus instead of obliging the Communists to really practice
their own politics of a left union and instead of clearly
posing the political problem, the Socialists have only helped
to obscure the issue.

Can it be said that this was the price of American aid?
But there again forthrightness could have been a force. The
question should have been raised publicly, an informed public opinion should have weighed in the negotiations with
America. Instead of that, we do not even know, three days
after Molotov's departure, precisely which point caused his
walk-out, and whether the Marshall Plan establishes American control over Europe. On this *Humanité*[7] is as vague as
the *Aube*.[8] Contemporary politics is truly an arena in which
questions are badly put, or put in such a way that one cannot side with either of the two present contestants. We are
called to choose between them. Our duty is to do no such
thing, to demand enlightenment from this side and that
side, to explain the maneuvers, to dissipate the myths. Like
everyone else we know that our future depends upon world
politics. We are neither on the same level nor below the level
of the mob. But we are in France and we cannot confound

7 Daily newspaper of P.C.F., Parti Communist Français (Translator).
8 Daily newspaper of M.R.P., Mouvement Républicain Populaire (Translator).

our future either with that of the U.S.S.R. or the American empire. The criticisms just leveled at French communism do not in themselves imply any allegiance to "Western" politics as it has developed in the last two months. It will be necessary to examine whether the U.S.S.R. has deprived herself of a plan acceptable to her, or whether, on the contrary, she has had to defend herself against some diplomatic attack or, finally, whether the Marshall Plan is not a mixture of peaceful intention and warlike deception and how, given this hypothesis, a peaceful politics could be possible. Democracy and liberty in practice demand above all that diplomatic maneuvers and countermaneuvers be subject to public opinion. At home and abroad, freedom and democracy assume that war is not inevitable because there is neither democracy nor freedom in war.

Such (partly abridged, partly in summary) are the reflections on the problem of violence which, when published this winter[9] earned the author replies which were also violent. We would not mention these critics here were it not that they have something to teach us about the Communist problem. After hardly a third of our study had appeared, and notice given of its continuation, some fellows who are not used to polemics, or have lost the habit, rushed to their desks and composed refutations motivated by moral disapproval but without a trace of clarity, at times attributing to us the very opposite of what we said and ignoring for the rest the problem which we tried to raise.

They have it that we said the Party cannot make errors.

---

[9] The present volume contains in addition Chapter III and other unpublished material.

We wrote that this was not a Marxist notion.[10] According to them, we said that the conduct of the revolution should be restored to an "initiated elite"; we are reproached with wanting to curb men under the law of a "transcendental *praxis*" that would eliminate human freedom with its spontaneity and risks. What we said is that this is Hegel but not Marx.[11] We are accused of "adoring" History. It is precisely this "adoration of an unknown god"[12] that we criticized in Koestler's version of communism. We argued that the dilemma of conscience and politics—commitment or refusal, fidelity or lucidity—imposes one of those heart-rending choices which Marx had not envisaged and which introduces a crisis into Marxist dialectics.[13] We are supposed to have said it was an example of Marxist dialectic. They remind us of Lenin's gentleness toward his political opponents. We in fact said that the terrorism of the trials is unparalleled in the Leninist period.[14] We showed how a conscientious Communist, such as Bukharin, can pass from revolutionary violence to today's communism—and ends by seeing that communism has denatured itself en route. They catch on to the first point. They refuse to read what follows.[15]

It is true, our study is lengthy and indignation cannot stand to wait. But these sensitive people, not content to cut

10 *Les Temps Modernes,* No. 13, October 1946, p. 10. (See p. 15 below.)

11 *Les Temps Modernes,* No. 16, February 1947, p. 688. (See p. 150 below.)

12 *Les Temps Modernes,* No. 13, p. 11. (See p. 16 below.)

13 Les Temps Modernes, No. 16, p. 686. (See p. 145 below.)

14 *Ibid.,* p. 682. (See p. 140 below.)

15 They even hide from the reader that there is a sequel. When it appeared, the *Révue de Paris* dishonestly wrote that we were publishing "a new study."

off our discourse, falsify what we have very clearly said at
the start. What we said was that, whether guilty or disinterested, the behavior of the collaborator—whether Pétain,
Laval, or Pucheu—leads to the Militia, the suppression of
the *maquis,* the execution of Politzer, and is responsible for
them. They have it that we said it is lawful to punish those
who have *done nothing.* We said that a revolution does not
define crimes according to the established law but in accordance with the law of the society which it wishes to
create. They say we said that the revolution does not judge
acts which have been committed but possible acts.

We argued that since he is concerned to govern others,
political man cannot complain of being judged for acts
whose consequences others must bear, nor of the often in-
exact image they form of him. We suggest that every man
who undertakes *to play a role* carries around him, as Diderot
said of the actor on stage, a "great fantom" in which he is
forever hidden, and he is responsible for his role even when
he cannot find in it what he wanted to be. In the eyes of
others the politician is never as he sees himself, not only
because others judge him rashly, but because they are not
him, and what for him is an error or negligence may be for
them absolute evil, slavery, or death. In accepting the chance
of glory in the role of politician, he accepts also the risk of
infamy, in either case "undeserved." Political action is of
its nature impure, because it is the action of one person upon
another and because it is collective action. An opponent
thinks he will make use of the kulaks; a leader thinks of
using the ambition of those around him in order to save

his work. If they are supported by the forces which they unleash, there they stand before history, the man of the kulaks, and the man of a clique. There is no politician who can flatter himself upon his innocence. To govern, it has been said, is to foresee, and the politician cannot excuse himself for what he has not foreseen. Yet, there is always the unforeseeable. There is the tragedy.

Thereupon they speak of an "apology for the Moscow Trials." But when we say that there are no innocents in politics that applies much more to the judges than to the condemned. We ourself have not said that it was necessary to condemn Bukharin nor that the Trials were justified by Stalingrad.[16] Even on the supposition that Stalingrad would have been impossible without Bukharin's death, no one in 1937 could foresee the train of events which on this hypothesis would lead from the one to the other, for the simple reason that there is no science of the future. Victory cannot justify the Trials at the time and, consequently, never, since it was not certain that they were indispensable to victory. If oppression runs on other lines than these uncertainties, it is out of passion and no passion has the assurance of being pure: there is the devotion to the Soviet experiment, but also police sadism, envy, servility toward power, the pitiable joy of being strong. Oppression rallies all these forces just as opposition confounds the honorable and the sordid. Why

16 In support of our interpretation of Bukharin we have quoted a recent remark of Stalin which to some extent renders justice to the convicted. That closes the debate, in our view. Of course, this refers only to the debate over the "charges" of espionage and sabotage.

should it be necessary to hide what there was of Soviet patriotism in the purges when one reveals what honor there was in the opposition?

That is going too far, we shall be told. This impassioned justice is nothing but a crime. There is only one justice, for moments of calm and for others. In 1917, Pétain did not ask the mutineers whom he had shot what were the "motives" for their "opposition." All the same, the liberals did not cry out against barbarism. The troops marched past the dead bodies. The music played. We certainly have no intention of embroiling ourselves in ceremonial proprieties, but we do not see why if it is grandiose when it is in the national defense it should become shameful in defense of the revolution. After so much exhortation to "Die for the Fatherland" we might well hear a "Die for the Revolution." After that the only question which remains is whether Bukharin really died for a revolution or a new humanity. That question is the one we have considered.

Such is our "apology." The critics then reply: you justify "tyranny of any kind," you teach that "the powers that be are always right," you provide "once for all a good conscience for future Grand Inquisitors . . ." They should learn how to read. We said that every legal system begins by being a power *de facto*. That does not mean that all power *de facto* is legitimate. We said that a policy cannot be justified by its good intentions. Still less can it be justified by barbarous intentions. We have never said that any policy which succeeds is good. We said that in order to be good a policy must succeed. We have never said that success justifies everything. We said that failure is a fault and in politics one does not have the right to make errors and that only success can turn what was at first audacity and faith into solid reason. The curse of politics is precisely that it must translate values into the order of facts. At the level of action, every desire is as good as foresight and, reciprocally, every prognostic is a kind of complicity. A policy therefore cannot be grounded in principle, it must also comprehend the facts of the situation. It was said long ago that politics is the art of the possible. That does not suppress our initiative: since we do not *know* the future, we have only, after carefully weighing everything, to push in our own direction. But that reminds us of the gravity of politics; it obliges us, instead of simply forcing our will, to look hard among the facts for the shape they should take.

Another accuses us of justifying a victorious Hitler. We do not justify anything or anyone. Since we acknowledge an element of chance in the most deliberate policy and thus an element of imposture in every "great man," we are far from acquitting anyone. We would rather say they are all unjustifiable. As for Hitler, even if he had won, he would have remained the wretch he was and the resistance to Nazism would have lost none of its validity. We are simply saying that to constitute a policy Nazism would have had to provide itself with a new vocabulary of order, to discover for itself actual justifications, to insinuate itself into existing forces; failing this, after fifty years of Nazism, there would remain nothing but a memory. A legal order that does not find the means of validating itself perishes with time; not that the one which succeeds it is thereby holy and venerable but because henceforth the new legal order constitutes the source of beliefs for the most part unquestioned which only a hero would dare contest. Though we have never subordinated the state of validity to the existing state we have refused to locate it in a nonexistent state.

We say that "there is no one destined to win, choose at your own risk." The critics understand this as "run before the conqueror." We say, "all law is violence." They understand "all violence is legitimate." We say "the facts are never an excuse, it is your consent which makes them irrevocable." They take this as "let us adore the facts." We say "history is cruel." They make of it "history is adorable." They make us say that the Grand Inquisitor is absolved the moment we deny him the only justification he can tolerate; namely, a superhuman science of the future. *The contingency of the future, which accounts for the violent acts of those in power, by the same token deprives these acts of all legitimacy, or equally legitimates the violence of their opponents.* The right of the opposition is exactly equal to the right of those in power.

If our critics cannot see this reasoning and think that our essay contains arguments against liberty, that is because for them one is already speaking against liberty when one says that it involves the risk of illusion and failure. We argue that an action can produce something else than it envisaged, but nevertheless political man assumes its consequences. Our critics want no such harsh conditions. They need a black and white line between the guilty and the innocent. They do not understand that there are traps in sincerity or any ambiguity in political life. One of them, in summing us up, wrote with obvious indignation: "the fact of killing: good at one moment, bad at another . . . The criterion of action is not in the action itself." Such indignation is a proof of fine sentiments but not much reading. For did not Pascal three centuries ago bitterly remark that it has become honorable to kill a man if he lives on the other side of the river, and conclude that things are such that these absurdities are the life of societies? We shall not go so far. We are saying one could take this road if it was to create a society without violence. Another critic persuades himself that in *Darkness at Noon* Koestler "takes the side of the innocent against an unjust or misguided judge." This is a simple admission of not having read the book. For heaven's sake, it is surely not a case of *judicial error*. For then we would still be in the happy universe of liberalism where one knows what one is doing and where, at least, one always keeps his conscience. The greatness of Koestler's book is precisely that it leads us to see that Rubashov does not always know how to evaluate his conduct and, at various moments, approves of it and condemns it. His judges are not impulsive or ill-informed men. It is much more serious: they know he is honest, yet they condemn him from political duty because they believe in the socialist future of the U.S.S.R. He himself knows he is honest (as far as one can be) and accuses himself because he has always believed in the revolution. Our critics cannot handle these torments or doubts. They bravely repeat that an innocent is an innocent, a murderer is a murderer. Montaigne said, "the public good demands that one betrays, lies and massacres. . . ." He described political man caught in the alternative of doing nothing or of being a criminal: "What is the remedy? There is no remedy, if he really was caught between these two extremes he would still have to act; but if he did so without regret, if it did not weigh upon him it is a sign that he is not in good conscience." Montaigne therefore already understood political man as an unhappy consciousness. Our critics do not want to know anything of that sort; they need a liberty that keeps a good conscience; they want plainspeaking without its consequences.

In this there is a true *regression* of political thought in the psychoanalytic sense of a childhood regression. They are trying to forget a problem which has troubled Europe since the Greeks, namely, that the human condition may be such that it has no happy solution. Does not every action involve us in a game which we cannot entirely control? Is there not a sort of evil in collective life? At least in times of crisis, does not each freedom encroach upon the freedom of others? Forced to choose between action and respect for consciences which are mutually exclusive and yet solicit one another, if the respect is to be meaningful and the action humane, is not our choice always good and always bad? Even though our political life creates a civilization we can never renounce, does it not also contain a fundamental disease? For though it does not prevent us from distinguishing between political systems or from preferring one to another, it does prevent us from concentrating all criticism upon a single system and thus it "relativizes" political judgment.

These questions only sound new to those who have read nothing or have forgotten everything. The trial and death of Socrates would not have remained a subject of reflection and commentary if it had only been an incident in the struggle of evil men against good men and had one not seen in it an innocent man who accepts his sentence, a just man who obeys conscience and yet refuses to reject the world and obeys the *polis,* meaning that it belongs to man to judge the law *at the risk of being judged by it.* It is the nightmare of an involuntary responsibility and guilt by circumstance which already underlies the Oedipus myth: Oedipus did not want to marry his mother nor kill his father but he did it and what he did stands as a crime. The whole of Greek tragedy assumes this idea of an essential contingency through which we are all guilty and all innocent because we do not know what we are doing. Hegel has admirably expressed the impartiality of the hero who can see well that his adversaries are not necessarily "wretches," everyone being right in a sense, and accomplishes his task without hoping for everyone's approval, nor his own entirely.[17] The myth of the sorcerer's apprentice is another of those obsessive images in which from time to time the West expresses its terror of being overwhelmed by nature and history. There are Christian critics who now blithely dissociate themselves from the Inquisition because they are threatened by a Communist Inquisition—overlooking that Christianity has not condemned the principle of the Inquisition and was even

---

[17] Between this hero and the Innocent whose edifying image is offered to us these days, the difference is roughly that between real soldiers and soldiers described in the *Echo de Paris.* When our older brothers in the 1914 war were demobilized their right-thinking families welcomed them in phrases from Barrès. I remember those silences, the tense atmosphere, and my childlike surprise when the soldier covered in palms of glory turned his face and refused the eulogy. As Alain said a little later, it was because behind it lay hate, with fear, and before it courage, with forgiveness. They knew that there is no line between good people and the rest and that, in war, the most honorable causes prove themselves by means that are not honorable.

able, during the war, to profit here and there from the secular arm. How can they ignore that the Inquisition is focused on the suffering of an innocent man, that the bully "does not know what he is doing" and so is right in his way, or that it is in this way that conflict is solemnly fixed in the heart of History?

The sense of this conflict finds its sharpest expression in Max Weber's sociology. Max Weber refuses to choose between an "ethics of responsibility," which does not judge according to the intention of the action but according to its consequences, and an "ethics of faith" or "conscience," which places value on the unconditional respect for ends regardless of consequences. Being no Machiavelli, he refuses to sacrifice the ethics of faith. Yet, he also refuses to sacrifice the result apart from which action loses all meaning. There is a "polytheism" and "struggle of the gods."[18] Weber criticizes equally political realism, which often chooses too soon in order to spare itself effort, and the ethics of faith, with its *Hier stehe ich, ich kann nicht anders,*[19] to which it resorts in the face of an inescapable dilemma but which is only a heroic formula guaranteeing man neither the efficacy of his action nor even the approval of others or himself.

In Weber's view, ethics is Kant's categorical imperative or the Sermon on the Mount. But to treat one's fellow as an end not as a means is a commandment strictly inapplicable in any concrete politics (even if one's goal is a society in which this rule will become a reality). By definition, politics combines means

[18] R. Aron, *La Sociologie allemande contemporaine.* Paris, F. Alcan, 1935, p. 122.
[19] *Ibid.*

and calculates consequences. But among the consequences are human reactions which are therefore treated as natural phenomena; again, the means are, at least partially, human actions reduced to the level of instruments. As for Christ's ethic, to "turn the other cheek" involves a lack of dignity, unless it is saintliness, and saintliness is out of place in the life of collectivities. Politics is in essence unethical. It contains "a pact with the powers of hell" because it is the struggle for power and power leads to violence over which the state has a legitimate monopoly. . . . There is more than rivalry between the gods, there is an inexpiable struggle.[20]

That is how Raymond Aron in 1938 was able to express a view that was not his own but which he considered to be at least one of the more serious views without anyone accusing him of toadying Nazi or Communist power which, as is well known, would not have been without appeal.

Those were happy days. People still knew how to read. One could still think aloud. All that seems to be over now. The war has so drained everyone, demanded so much patience, so much courage, has so multiplied glorious as well as inglorious horrors that men no longer have the energy even to look violence in the face, to see it at its source. They have so longed to be rid at last of the presence of death and to return to peace that they cannot bear to see it still elude them; a slightly frank view of history is therefore taken by them as an apology for violence. They cannot bear the thought of still being exposed to violence, of still having to pay with courage to exercise liberty. Although everything

[20] R. Aron, *Essai sur la théorie de l'histoire dans l'allemagne contemporaine: la philosophie critique de l'histoire.* Paris, J. Vrin, 1938, pp. 266–267.

in politics as in the theory of knowledge shows that the reign of universal reason is problematic, that reason like liberty has to be made in a world not predestined to it, they prefer to forget experience, to drop culture there and solemnly formulate as venerable truths the tired sayings which answer their weariness. An innocent is an innocent, a culprit is a culprit, murder is murder—these are the conclusions of three thousand years of philosophy, meditation, theology, and casuistry. It would be too painful to have to admit that, in a way, the Communists, as well as their opponents are right. "Polytheism" is too difficult. So they choose the god of the East or the god of the West. And—it is always the same—precisely because it is out of weakness that they love peace, there they are, all ready for propaganda and war. In the last analysis, the truth from which they are running is that man has no rights over the world, that he is not, to talk like Sartre, "man by divine right," that he is thrown into an adventure whose happy end is not guaranteed any more than the harmony of mind and will assured in principle.

These remarks are true only of the better ones. If this were the place to go into details, we would describe the others. Their names are unimportant, for our purpose is entirely sociological. One critic in his defense of innocence becomes quite moving until the careful reader notices that his plea does not say a word about the innocents with whom Koestler is concerned and whom we have studied, namely, the opposition condemned at Moscow. "I consider it," he says, "deplorable that these discussions are tied to the Russian example and problem: we understand it so poorly."

Here we have a very astute innocence. He firmly refuses help to Bukharin, who may well need it, and reserves it for Joan of Arc and the Duke of Enghien who have turned to dust. This knight errant is very prudent. He puts us, or very nearly so, among the "flatterers of power." We would ask whether one pleases the Communists more by speaking about the Moscow Trials as we have done or by avoiding them as he does. From all appearances, he is primarily interested in French purity and "the double scandal of abusive oppression and unthinkable immunity." Of course, we have never said a word in favor of abusive oppression. We did say that a disinterested collaborator is no less guilty and that in extreme circumstances political man risks his neck even if he is neither greedy nor corrupt. This is the idea that no one wants to see or to discuss. No one wants politics to be something serious or nothing but that. What they are defending in the end is the irresponsibility of political man. And not without reason.

The writer who before the war and even a little later saw more Ministers in a week than we expect to see in a lifetime would not know how to tolerate seriousness in politics, far less tragedy. When we say that political decision contains a risk of error and that only events can show whether we were right, he understands this *as best he can* to mean "to be right means to be in power, to be on the side of right." That carries a signature. To find such words they have to be a part of you. A shallow man who needs a shallow world in which nothing would be irreparable, speaks on behalf of eternal justice. It is the scoundrel who defends "rigid ethics." It is Péguy who defends ethical flexibility.

There are no more rigid educators than parents. To the very extent that a man is unsure of himself or lacks gravity and, in our terms, true morality, he reserves in the depths of himself a sanctuary of principles which, in Marx's words, provide him with a "spiritual *point d'honneur*," a "general basis of consolation and justification." The same critic goes to pains to rediscover this warning as far back as Saint-Just and credits the Revolutionary Tribunal with "parodies of debate . . . the homage that . . . vice pays virtue out of hypocrisy." That is just the way our fathers used to reason— libertines in practice, unmovable over principle. It was a double life that they offered us in the name of ethics and culture. They had no desire to find themselves alone and naked before an enigmatic world. Let them have their peace. They did what they could. We might even add that this blackguardism was not without its sweetness since it disguised what was disturbing in our condition. But when one picks up a moral loudspeaker to preach it and in the name of fraudulent certainties questions the honesty of those who want to understand what they are doing we reply gently but firmly: mind your own business.

Finally, it may be wondered why we give ourself so much trouble. If in the end we believe that one cannot be a Communist nor sacrifice liberty to Soviet society, why do we go through so many detours to arrive at this conclusion? It is because the sense of the conclusion is not the same if reached by one path or by another. It is—once again—because there are really two usages and even two ideas of liberty. There is a liberty which is the insignia of a clan and already the slogan of a propaganda. History is logical at least inasmuch as certain ideas have a pre-established affinity with certain politics or interests because each of them presupposes the same conception of man. There is already a warlike attitude involved in democratic liberties taken as the sole criterion of judgment upon societies, or in democracies absolved of all the violence they perpetrate here and there because they recognize and at least internally practice the principles of liberty—in short, in liberty which has paradoxically become a principle of separation and pharisaism. On the contrary, one will never extract a propaganda from an active liberty which seeks to understand other men and reunites all of us. Many writers are already living in a state of war. They see themselves already shot. When this essay first appeared in *Les Temps Modernes* a friend came to us and said: "In any case, even if enlightened Communists think roughly what you have said of the trials, you say it whereas they hide it and you therefore deserve the firing-squad." We graciously granted him this conclusion which involves no difficulty. But what next? The possibility that a system might condemn us does not prove its absolute evil nor exempt us from doing it justice when there is occasion. If we accustom ourselves to see in it nothing but a menace to our own life, we get into a struggle to the death to which all means are good—myth, propaganda, the game of violence. From such deadly perspectives one does not reason well. We have to understand once and for all that these things can happen—and think like living men.

Perhaps this essay already comes too late and everyone's mind is already set on war. Our mistake, if that is what it is, has been to follow, pen in hand, a discussion that began a

long time ago among young comrades and to hand in the
result to every kind of fanatic. Recently someone[21] asked,
for whom does one write? That is a profound question. One
should always dedicate a book. Not that one alters one's
thoughts with a change of interlocutor, but because every
word, whether we know it or not, is always a word with
someone, which presupposes a certain degree of esteem or
friendship, the resolution of a certain number of misunder-
standings, the transcendence of a certain latent content and,
finally, the appearance of a part of the truth in the encounters we live. Certainly, we were not writing for sec-
tarians but neither for the colleague so superior and so much
in search of himself. We were writing for friends whose
names we would gladly inscribe here were it permissible to
make witnesses of the dead. They were simple, they had no
reputation, no ambition, no political past. One could talk
with them. After the Nazi-Soviet pact in 1939 one of them
said to us: "I have no philosophy of history." Another one
refused to acknowledge this episode in any way. Yet, with
all the reservations imaginable, they joined up again with
the Communists during the war. The episode had not
changed them. The first one, after his men had been taken
prisoner by the militiamen, went into the village to share
their fate since he could do nothing more for them. The
other person was locked in the Dépôt for two months, and
when called, as everyone thought, to appear before a French
tribunal, she wrote that she would reject her lawyers if
they tried to plead her case on grounds of her youth. Per-

---

[21] Jean-Paul Sartre, *What is Literature?* Translated by Bernard Frechtman,
New York, Philosophical Library, 1949.

haps it will be allowed of them that they were individuals and that they understood what liberty is. Then it will not seem strange if we, who have to speak about communism, search in darkness and mist for those faces that have gone from the earth.

Part One: Terror

I. Koestler's Dilemmas

"THAT IS WHAT they want to set up in France," exclaimed an anti-Communist after reading *Darkness at Noon*.[1] "How exciting it must be to live under this regime!" exclaimed a sympathizer of Russian origin who had emigrated in 1905. The first character has forgotten that all regimes are criminal, that Western liberalism rests upon the forced labor of the colonies and twenty wars, that from an ethical standpoint the death of a Negro lynched in Louisiana, or of a native in Indonesia, Algeria, or Indochina is no less excusable than Rubashov's death; he forgets that communism does not invent violence but finds it already institutionalized, that for the moment the question is not to know whether one accepts or rejects violence, but whether the violence with which one is allied is "progressive" and tends toward its own suspension or toward self-perpetuation; and, finally, that in order to decide this question the crime has to be set in the logic of a situation, in the dynamics of

[1] Arthur Koestler, *Darkness at Noon,* Translated by Daphne Hardy, London, Jonathan Cape, 1940. All quotations are from this English translation rather than the French edition used by Merleau-Ponty (Translator).

a regime and into the historical totality to which it belongs, instead of judging it by itself according to that morality mistakenly called "pure" morality.

The second character has forgotten that violence—anguish, pain, and death—is only appealing in imagination, in art and written history. The most peaceloving men are able to speak of Richelieu and Napoleon without a shudder. One should try to imagine how Urbain Grandier saw Richelieu and how the Duc d'Enghien viewed Napoleon. The remoteness and inertia of past events transforms a crime into an historical necessity and casts a pale shadow over the victim. But which one of Richelieu's academic admirers would kill Urbain Grandier with his own hands? What administrator would himself kill the natives whose deaths he brings about in building a colonial railroad? But the past and what is distant have been and are still lived by men who had and still have only one life to live and the screams of a single man condemned to death are unforgettable.

The anti-Communist refuses to see that violence is universal while the exalted sympathizer refuses to see that no one can look violence in the face. Neither one of them could have read *Darkness at Noon* carefully if he opposes these two facts. Even if it does not pose the question properly, the book raises the problem of our times. That is enough for it to have aroused a lively interest. It is also enough for it to have been not properly *read,* because the questions which haunt us are precisely those which we refuse to formulate. Let us then try to understand this famous but poorly understood book.

Rubashov always dealt with external things and historical processes. It would have been difficult for him to have had to determine his own conduct: the fate of other men as well as his personal destiny unfolded before him, in the world of things, in the making of the Revolution, its success and its spread. What was he beyond a certain X upon whom were imposed tasks clearly called for by the situation? Not even the danger of death could bring him to withdraw into himself: to a revolutionary a man's death is not the end of a world but an agency which cancels itself out. Death is only a particular instance or an extreme limit of historical inactivity and that is why revolutionaries do not say that an adversary has died but that he has been "suppressed physically." For Rubashov and his comrades the "I" was both so unreal and so indecent that they ridiculed it by referring to it as the "grammatical fiction." Humanity, values, virtues, the mutual reconciliation of men, were not in their opinion ends to be reached by reason but possibilities of the proletariat which it was a matter of bringing to power.

For years then Rubashov had lived in ignorance of the subjective. It matters little that Richard is a long-standing and devoted militant, if he weakens, if he disputes the official line, he will be expelled. It is not a question of knowing whether or not the dockers want to unload the oil sent by the homeland of the Revolution to a reactionary government: by prolonging the boycott, the country of the Revolution would risk losing a market. Their industrial development counts for more than the consciousness of the masses. The leaders of the dockers' cell will be expelled. For his own part Rubashov treats himself no better than the others. He believes that the Party leadership is mistaken and he says so. Once arrested, he disavows his oppositionist standpoint, not to save his life, but to save his political life and to stick within history where he has always been. One may wonder how he could love Arlova. Indeed, it is a strange love. Once only she tells him, "You can always do with me whatever you want." And never anything more. Not a word from her when she is broken by the Party cell. Not a word from her the evening she visits Rubashov. And not a word from Rubashov in her defense. He only speaks of her to denounce her when asked by the Party. Honor, dishonor, sincerity, falsehood—such words have no meaning for the man of history. There is only *objective* treason and *objective* merit. The traitor is he who *in fact* deserts the country of the Revolution as it stands, its leadership and its institutions. All the rest is psychology.

When despised, psychology avenges itself; the individual and the state, once confounded in the early stages of the Revolution, later reappear in confrontation. The masses are no longer the vehicle of the state, they are its subjects. Decisions are no longer submitted to discussion throughout the Party, they are imposed through discipline. Unlike in the beginning of the Revolution, policy is no longer based upon a continuous analysis of the world revolutionary movement, nor is it seen any more as the direct extrapolation of the spontaneous course of history. The theoreticians run after the decisions reached on the basis of power in order to rationalize them despite the indifference of power. Bit by bit Rubashov becomes acquainted with that subjectivity which stands back from events and evaluates them. Arrested once more, and this time cut off from action and historical events, it is not just the voices of the masses and the rejected militants that he believes he hears: even his class enemy takes on a human shape for him once more. The reactionary officer who occupies the cell next to his—a woman's man, infatuated with honor and personal courage—is no longer just one of the White Guards whom Rubashov had shot during the Revolution, but *someone to whom one can talk* by tapping on the wall in the language of prisoners everywhere in the world. For the first time Rubashov sees the Revolution from the standpoint of the White Guard and he realizes that no one can feel justified in the eyes of those on whom he has inflicted violence. He "understands" the White Guards' hate, he "forgives," but, from then on, even his revolutionary past is in question. And yet it was precisely in order to liberate men that he had used violence against some men. He does not think he was wrong. But he is no longer innocent. There remain all those considerations which it was necessary to neglect. There remains another claim than that of history and the revolutionary enterprise, another criterion than that of reason absorbed in the calculation of efficacy. There remains the need to undergo what one has made others submit to in order to re-establish with them a reciprocity and communication to which revolutionary action does not accommodate itself. Rubashov is to die in opposition, and in silence, like all those whom he executed in his own day.

All the same, if it is men who matter, why should he be more faithful to the dead than to the living? Outside of prison, there are all those who, for better or worse, are fol-

lowing the path on which Rubashov set them. If he dies in
silence, he abandons these men with whom he has fought
and his death will not enlighten them. Moreover, what
other path is there to show them? Perhaps what is happen-
ing is that more and more and bit by bit we have arrived at
a new politics. To break with the regime would mean dis-
owning the revolutionary past to which he owes his origins.
Yet every time he thinks of 1917 it is clear to Rubashov that
the Revolution was necessary and that in the same circumstances he would be part of it, even knowing where it leads.
If one takes on the past, one must also take on the present.
To die in silence Rubashov would have had first to change
his morality—he would have had to prefer the vertigo of
"testimony," to prefer the immediate and crazy affirmation
of values to action in the world and upon history. Testimony
before whom? All during his youth he had learned that to
resort to this superterrestrial pleading was the most subtle
of mystifications, since it authorizes us to forsake men as
they are and makes us abandon an effective morality for an
ethereal ethics. He had learned that true morality laughs at
morality, that the only way of remaining true to values is to
turn outward in order to attain, as Hegel says, "the reality
of the moral idea," and that the short cut of spontaneous
feeling is the way of immorality. It was in the name of historical exigencies that he formerly defended dictatorship
and the violence it inflicted upon beautiful souls.[2] What
could he say today in reply to anyone relating his speeches
to him? Would it be that formerly dictatorship based its

[2] Hegel, *The Phenomenology of Mind*, London, George Allen and Unwin Ltd.,
1949, pp. 642–679.

decisions upon a theoretical analysis and a free discussion of viewpoints? That is true. But, once the line was chosen, it was necessary to obey, and for those who do not see clearly, the dictatorship of truth is no different from sheer force. Once one has defended the former, one has to accept the latter. And what if the very hardening of the dictatorship and the renunciation of theory were imposed by the world situation? Rubashov would give in.

As soon as he returns to the hard Marxist rule which demands that a man be described not by his intentions but by what he does, and that action be evaluated not according to its subjective meaning but its objective sense, then again the pattern of Rubashov's life is transformed. First of all, because some thoughts and words, which taken singly remain in the indeterminacy of the subjective, now reinforce one another and form a coherent system. The testimony on the stand is very far from being false. Rubashov even remarks on the meticulous reporting of certain events and conversations. If there is any falsehood it lies in this very preciseness and in fixing once and for all on paper a phrase or an idea born of the moment. But is even that a distortion? It is not unjust to impute to Rubashov certain sarcastic remarks and amusing comments but also what became of them in the minds of the young people listening to him and who, being less tired than him and more true than him to his youth, took his thoughts to their practical conclusion, to the point of conspiracy. After all, Rubashov says to himself, looking at the young man accusing him, perhaps he is the truth of which I was thinking.

Rubashov never recommended terrorism and when he

spoke of using violence against the Party leadership, he only
meant political violence. But political violence means arrests,
and what happens when he who is arrested defends himself? Rubashov was never in the pay of a foreign country.
But since he had thought vaguely of overthrowing the Party
leadership he should at least have foreseen the reaction of
neighboring countries and perhaps to have disarmed it in
advance. Thus there was that brief conversation with a foreign diplomat in which no deal was concluded, in which
everything was conditional and kept very tentative, but
where the price of a friendly neutrality was nevertheless
indicated. Of course, to Rubashov it was only a matter of
eventually sacrificing a province in order to save the future
of the Revolution; but for the foreign diplomat it was a
matter of weakening and dismembering the country of the
Revolution. Who can say which of the two calculations was
right in the end, and whether in the last analysis and before
history, Rubashov would have been the savior or the ruin
of the Revolution? Moreover, since history is polarized and
the dynamics of the class struggle involve the interpretation
of every event in favor of one or the other side, there can be
no room for neutral or indifferent actions, for even silence
plays its role and the shifts between intention and action,
self and the other, opposition and treason are unnoticeable.
Finally, *once he has been arrested,* Rubashov the opposition
member *becomes* in truth a traitor. By the fact of having
been beaten, the opposition confesses its inability to establish a new revolutionary leadership. Historically, it amounts
to nothing more than an attempt against the only possible
revolutionary leadership and thus it becomes counterrevolu-

tionary and treasonable. The results of the attempt work back upon its origins and reveal its total significance.

If Rubashov had wished to invoke his own intentions against this mode of objective thinking, he would have been calling to his aid a philosophy which he had always denied. How could he reject the judgment of the new generation which he had helped to form and which practiced objective thinking to the very limit? After all, it is Rubashov who judges Rubashov through the voice of Gletkin. That is why in the end he will sign the "false" confessions prepared by Gletkin. At first he pleaded guilty of having adopted an *objectively* counterrevolutionary position. It was to be understood that his intentions remained revolutionary. If he let Gletkin "dot the i's" and translate into a conspiracy what was only a self-criticism of the Party and the regime, at least he refused to confess to being a spy and a saboteur.

But this last defense was removed. Revolutionary honor itself is only a species of bourgeois dignity. Rubashov belongs to a generation which believed it could restrict violence to the enemies of the proletariat, treat the proletariat and its representatives humanely, and save one's personal honor through devotion to the Revolution. That is because he and his comrades were intellectuals born in comfortable circumstances and brought up in a prerevolutionary culture. They were eight or nine years old when they were given their first watch. They were unaware that their values presupposed a certain state of freedom and comfort and were completely meaningless apart from it. They had not experienced need and necessity. For himself, Gletkin was sixteen years old when he learned that the hour is divided into sixty minutes.

He was born among the peasants who now work in the factories. He knows that they cannot be let free if one wants them to work and that a legal system remains purely nominal as long as its material basis has not been established. Between Rubashov and Gletkin there is the difference between a political generation which by chance had shared the cultural privileges of the bourgeoisie and a generation commissioned to spread culture universally, but first to establish its economic foundations. The distinction between the subjective and the objective, familiar to Rubashov, is however ignored by Gletkin. Gletkin stands for humanity conscious of its material roots; he is the realization of what Rubashov had always spoken. *Objective* sabotage, *objective* treason—intentions notwithstanding—still belongs to the language of an earlier culture or to tomorrow's culture. Under the present circumstances, the inward man no longer exists, or not yet, and thus one can suppress this misleading distinction. One has to surrender.

But Rubashov is not yet finished with himself. While he was speaking before the tribunal, accusing himself and bringing dishonor upon himself, he was still living within history. But there was still the test of the last days in prison to come. He had put himself in order with history, he had concluded his public life just as he had begun it and he had redeemed his past. But, for a while longer, he survived that life which he had already brought to a close. How could he without suppressing his own conscience or without becoming Gletkin, believe himself to have been a traitor and a saboteur? He himself is not universal history; he is Rubashov. He had managed for the last time to surrender himself

to history and to look like a traitor to the others, but he
could not possibly regard himself in the same way. From
the very fact of still being alive, he inevitably judges both
his own surrender, since he is the author of it, and the system which demands it. How then does he see his life at this
moment? Whether they realized it or not, he and his comrades had started from the affirmation of a value: the value
of men. One does not become a revolutionary through science, but out of indignation. Science comes afterward to fill
in and delimit that open protest. It taught Rubashov and his
companions that the liberation of man presupposed a socialist economy and so they set to work. But he learned that in
order to construct this economy in the particular circumstances of the land of the Revolution it was necessary to impose greater suffering than was known under the ancient
regime; that in order to free men in the future it was necessary to oppress men in the present. Once the work had
begun it established such forceful imperatives that all perspective was lost: "The work had lasted forty years, and
right at the start he had forgotten the question for whose
sake he had embarked on it."[3] The consciousness of self and
the other which had animated the enterprise at the start had
become entangled in the web of mediations separating existing humanity from its future fulfillment.

Having done everything that he had had to do, it is not at
all surprising that Rubashov is ready to *recover himself* and
to yield to that alien and as yet unknown experience for
him, which consists in the inner grasp of oneself as consciousness: as a being outside time and space, a light upon

[3] *Darkness at Noon*, p. 244.

which depends every appearance and every conceivable thing, and before which everything that happens, every sorrow and every joy is a matter of indifference—finally, as participation in an infinite. It is before this infinite that at the moment he feels accountable and guilty. Now that history is finished for him, he is following in the reverse direction the road traced by Hegel in the *Phenomenology* from death or from consciousness to History. Should he perhaps have abandoned the attempt to build a new state so as to remain faithful to the actual capacity of humanity? Perhaps it is better to act as a moral man and to bear witness daily to the inward man. "Perhaps it was not suitable for a man to think every thought to its logical conclusion."[4] "Perhaps it did not suit mankind to sail without ballast. And perhaps reason alone was a defective compass, which led one on such a winding, twisted course that the goal finally disappeared in the mist."[5] Shut up within this internal evidence, and thus disengaged from the world, Rubashov can no longer find any meaning in his behavior during the trial, nor in his death. Is it only now that he sees more clearly— or was it when he was in front of the tribunal? "He was a man who had lost his shadow, free from all impediments. . . ."

One may wonder what sense there is in reflecting on history when one no longer has any historical shadow, or in reflecting on life once one is shut out from it. Is it in life or before death that one understands life better? If he were suddenly set free and restored to the Party, how would he

4 *Ibid.*, p. 247.
5 *Ibid.*, p. 248.

continue his life, since while he disposed of it freely and up to the very last moments before the tribunal, he refused to speak in the accents of the inward man? Do Rubashov's last reflections yield us any different a formula for life than that which he followed while alive? Are they not rather the expression of subjectivity's irreducible protestation against an adventure with which it could never be reconciled, but to which it is committed for reasons that are forever valid? Even in his last hours Rubashov does not disavow the Revolution: "Perhaps the Revolution had come too early, an abortion with monstrous deformed limbs. Perhaps the whole thing had been a bad mistake in timing."[6] And perhaps, once the economic foundations were established, a society would be possible later in which the means would conform to the ends and the individual, instead of being cancelled in favor of the collective interest, would reunite with other individuals to constitute together an earthly infinity.[7] Even in the closing pages of the book, Koestler therefore does not exactly reach a conclusion. His personal conclusion is to be found elsewhere. *Darkness at Noon* limits itself to the description of a dialectical situation from which Rubashov does not break free even by force of the "oceanic feeling." It is the dialectic created by man's inability to find outside himself what inwardly he senses himself to be, and yet not to keep from looking outside himself for that very thing. Once humanism attempts to fulfill itself with any consistency it becomes transformed into its opposite, namely, into violence.

[6] *Ibid.*, p. 248.
[7] *Ibid.*, p. 249.

One is tempted to reply to Koestler that Marxism has actually transcended the alternatives in which Rubashov loses himself. And indeed there is very little Marxism in *Darkness at Noon,* whether in Rubashov's formulas, those of Gletkin, or those of Koestler once one looks into them. The solidarity of the individual with history which Rubashov and his comrades experienced in the revolutionary struggle gets translated into a mechanistic philosophy which disfigures it and is the source of the inhuman alternatives with which Rubashov finishes. To them, man is simply the reflection of his surroundings; the great man is the one whose ideas reflect most exactly the objective conditions of action; and history at least in principle is a rigorous science.

Perhaps later, much later, it would be taught by means of tables of statistics, supplemented by such anatomical sections. The teacher would draw on the blackboard an algebraic formula representing the conditions of life of the masses of a particular nation at a particular period: "Here, citizens, you see the objective factors which conditioned this process." And, pointing with his ruler to a gray foggy landscape between the second and third lobe of No. 1's brain, "Now you see the subjective reflection of these factors" . . .[8]

In ethics as in philosophy Rubashov and his comrades believed it was necessary to choose between inward and external values; either conscience is everything or else it is nothing:

There are only two conceptions of human ethics, and they are at opposite poles. One of them is Christian and humane,

[8] *Ibid.,* pp. 23–24.

declares the individual to be sacrosanct, and asserts that the rules of arithmetic are not to be applied to human units. The other starts from the basic principle that a collective aim justifies all means, and not only allows, but demands, that the individual should in every way be subordinated and sacrificed to the community—which may dispose of it as an experimentation rabbit or a sacrificial lamb.[9]

Here Rubashov and his comrades are following a sort of sociological scientism rather than anything in Marx. Political man is an engineer who employs means useful to achieving a given end. The logic which Rubashov follows is not the existential logic of history described by Marx and expressed in the inseparability of objective necessity and *the spontaneous movement of the masses;* it is the summary logic of the technician who deals only with inert objects which he manipulates as he pleases. Given that the goal to be achieved is the power of the proletariat, represented by the Party, individuals are simply the instruments of the Party. "The Party leadership is mistaken," a German militant tells Rubashov after the failure of the German revolution. "The Party can never be mistaken," said Rubashov. "You and I can make a mistake. Not the Party."[10] This would be a Marxist reply if it meant that resolutions taken after discussion are binding because they express the effective state of the Revolution in the world and the way that situation is experienced by the masses, and that consequently, in a Marxist philosophy of history, revolutions are the best

[9] *Ibid.,* p. 153.
[10] *Ibid.,* pp. 47–48.

possible testimony for the individual. But Rubashov's reply is in no way Marxist if it attributes a divine infallibility to the Party; since the Party has to *deliberate,* there can be no question of any geometric proof or any perfectly clear line. Since there are *detours* it shows that at certain moments the official line needs reconsideration and that if it were persisted in would lead to error.

In Rubashov's mind and in Koestler's version of communism, history is no longer what it was for Marx: the manifestation of human values through a process which might involve dialectical detours but at least could not entirely ignore human purposes. History is no longer the living element of man, the response to his wishes, the locus of revolutionary fraternity. It becomes an external force which has lost the sense of the individual and becomes the sheer force of fact. Hegel's famous saying that "The real is the rational and the rational is the real" is interpreted by Rubashov as an arbitrary justification of everything that exists in the name of a history that knows better than we do where it is going. The same formula did not stop Marx from preserving the role of consciousness in the achievement of the revolution and it generally serves Marxists as an invitation to understand the course of events and to modify events through understanding. Instead of the "real" becoming transparent to reason once it is understood, rationality effaces itself before the obscurity of what is real and judgment surrenders to the adoration of an unknown god. "History knows no scruples and no hesitation, inert and unerring, she flows towards her goal. At every bend in her course she leaves the mud which she carries and the corpses of the drowned. History knows her way. She makes no mistakes."[11] Marx himself had written:

It is not "history" which uses men as a means of achieving— as if it were an individual person—*its* own ends. History is *nothing* but the activity of men in pursuit of their ends.[12]

Evidently, Rubashov knows very well that no one can know anything but fragments of such a thoroughly deterministic History, that for everyone there are lacunae in this objectified History and no one can possess more than a "subjective image" of it which he is in no position to compare with an objectified History conceived as something far transcending humanity. But from the fact that an objectified History means nothing to us Koestler does not conclude that the realist myth should be abandoned. He simply projects it into the future and in the expectation of that happy day when we shall have knowledge of the whole of history, though a rigorous science abandons us to our disagreements and conflicts. It is only in a far-off future that science will be in a position to eliminate the subjective elements in our forecasts and to construct a thoroughly objective model of our relations with history. "Until this stage was reached, politics would remain bloody dilettantism, mere superstition and black magic."[13] This will be a gamble. "Meanwhile he is

[11] *Ibid.*, p. 48.

[12] *Karl Marx*, Selected Writings in Sociology and Social Philosophy. Edited and with an Introduction and Notes by T. B. Bottomore and M. Rubel, London, Watts & Co., 1956, p. 63.

[13] *Darkness at Noon*, p. 24.

bound to act on credit and to sell his soul to the devil, in the hope of history's absolution."[14]

Marxism had understood that it is inevitable that our understanding of history should be partial since every consciousness is itself historically situated. But instead of concluding that we are locked in our subjectivity and sworn to magic as soon as we try to act on the world, Marxism discovered, apart from scientific knowledge and its dream of impersonal truth, a new foundation for historical truth in the spontaneous logic of human existence, in the proletariat's self-recognition and the real development of the revolution. Marxism rested on the profound idea that human perspectives, however relative, are absolute because there is nothing else and no destiny. We grasp the absolute through our total *praxis,* if not through our knowledge—or, rather, men's mutual *praxis* is the absolute. Rubashov has no conception of the wisdom of Marxism, which comes from basing knowledge on *praxis,* which is in turn clarified by knowledge, or from the shaping of the proletariat by theoretical discussion that is in turn subject to the consent of the proletariat. He does not understand the art of the great Marxists of 1917 who deciphered history while it was taking place and projected its trends through decisions that avoided equally any subjective folly or *amor fati.* Rubashov has no other policy or any other interpretation of history with which to challenge the Party leadership; he has only the memory of Arlova, the image of Richard or Little Loewy— emotions, anxieties, and pangs of conscience which never disturb his basic faith in *the wisdom of the event.* But such

[14] *Ibid.,* p. 99.

a trust makes opinions useless and disarms Rubashov before he starts. He does not try to understand history; he simply waits for its judgment in fear and trembling.

> The horror which No. 1 emanated, above all consisted in the possibility that he was in the right . . .[15]

> And what if, after all, No. 1 were in the right? If here, in dirt and blood and lies, after all and in spite of everything, the grandiose foundations of the future were being laid? Had not history always been an inhumane, unscrupulous builder, mixing its mortar of lies, blood and mud?[16]

> But who will be proved right? It will only be known later.[17]

> There was certainty; only the appeal to that mocking oracle they called History, who gave her sentence only when the jaws of the appealer had long since fallen to dust.[18]

Like any form of masochism, this fascination with death and passion for obedience is ephemeral and ambiguous. Thus it can alternate the passion to command with shamelessly fine sentiments so that Rubashov is always on the point of switching from one attitude to the other and is always on the verge of treason. The original violence, which is the foundation of all other forms of violence, is that exerted by History when objectified as an incomprehensible Will before which all individual opinions are compounded as equally fragile hypotheses. Had Rubashov managed only once to criticize the notion of an entirely objective and

[15] *Ibid.*, p. 21.
[16] *Ibid.*, p. 126.
[17] *Ibid.*, p. 99.
[18] *Ibid.*, p. 22.

determinate history and realized that the only history we are
entitled to speak of is one whose image and future we ourselves construct by means of equally methodical and creative
interpretations, he would not have lost sight of the conjec-
tural nature of his and No. 1's opinions; he might then have
escaped the labyrinth of treason and renunciation. Far from
lending the individual the supporting weight of objectivity,
the scientistic myth discredits individual analysis in the name
of an ungraspable objective History and merely leaves the
individual oscillating between revolt and passivity.

One passage among all the others in *Darkness at Noon*
shows what little understanding Koestler has of Marxism. It
is where, after going back to his cell, Rubashov begins to
explain his confession in terms of the "theory of the relative
maturity of the masses." In a document addressed to the
Central Committee he shows that since every technical
progress makes the operation of the economy unintelligible
to the masses, the discussion and democracy which are possible at a lower level of development become impractical for
some time in a changing economy and can only be restored
much later when the masses have caught up with the inter-
vening changes and the objective conditions of production.
Whereas in a period of relative maturity it is the legitimate
task of the opposition to debate and appeal to the masses, in
a period of relative immaturity, it should simply toe the line.
It is clear what Koestler thinks of such reasoning. He cites
alongside it Machiavelli's teaching that words serve to disguise deeds, to excuse the disguise once it is discovered, in
addition to the famous saying from the Gospels according

to which the Christian should say *"Yea"* or *"Nay,"* anything else added being only the work of the devil. But this is to imply that Rubashov is systematically lying and afterward inventing good reasons for himself. It is also evidence that Marxist problems are not very well understood. The Marxist has recognized the mystification involved in the inner life; he lives in the world and in history. As he sees it, decision is not a private matter, it is not the spontaneous affirmation of those values we favor; rather, it consists in questioning our situation in the world, inserting ourselves in the course of events, in properly understanding and expressing the movement of history outside of which values remain empty words and have no other chance of realization. The difference between the adventurer who covers his retraction with theoretical pretexts and the Marxist who bases his commitment on a general thesis is that the former sets himself in the center of the world while the latter does not want to live outside of an intersubjective truth. Back in prison Rubashov constructs the theory of his confession with no dishonor to himself because his confession has its roots in the general situation of the home of the Revolution as he has reviewed in his conversation with Ivanov. All that might be said to Rubashov is that even this "objective" view of the historical situation is still one which he has endorsed; the individual cannot suppress the necessity of choosing, and even when he believes he is responding to what history expects of him, it is still he who interprets this expectation so that he can never displace his own responsibility; his view of the situation always involves the risk of error and partiality, so there is always the question of knowing whether he constructed his theory to make his peace with the Party because he found it hard to be alone.

Had Koestler limited himself to saying that there is a permanent risk of illusion and cowardice in any behavior which is based on the exigencies of the objective situation instead of on the abstract imperatives of subjective morality, there would have been something in what he says. But that would not constitute any condemnation of Marxism or any rehabilitation of moralism and the "beautiful soul." All one would have to reply is that, that is the way things are, human life is lived like this; Marxism expresses these facts and is not the cause of them; despite everything, we have to work without certainty and in confusion to uncover a truth. To confront Rubashov with the Christian absolute "Yea" or "Nay," or Kant's moral imperative, simply shows that one refuses to face the problem and falls back upon the attitudes of the holy will and the pharisee. It is necessary from the start to recognize *as a moral claim* the Communist's preoccupation with the role of objective factors and his wish to look upon himself from a standpoint both within and outside of history. One only has the right to point out the risks of "objective morality" if one also points out those of an ostentatious "subjective morality." In this instance, as in so many others, Koestler poses the problem in pre-Marxist terms. Marxism is neither the negation of subjectivity and human action nor the scientistic materialism with which Rubashov began. It is much more a theory of concrete subjectivity and concrete action—of subjectivity and action committed within a historical situation. Rubashov thinks he has discovered a mortal contradiction in the heart of Communist thought on fatalism and revolution.

> The individual stood under the sign of economic fatality, a wheel in a clockwork which had been wound up for all eternity and could not be stopped or influenced—and the Party demanded that the wheel should revolt against the clockwork and change its course.[19]

But who said that history is a clockwork and the individual a wheel? It was not Marx; it was Koestler. It is strange that in Koestler there is no inkling of the commonplace notion that by the very fact of its duration, history sketches the outline for the transformation of its own structures, changing and reversing its own direction because, in the last analysis men come to collide with the structures that alienate them inasmuch as economic man is also a human being. In short, Koestler has never given much thought to the simple idea of a dialectic in history.

However, the fact that Koestler is a mediocre Marxist does not release us from his questions: on the contrary, it raises them all the more sharply. Whatever the position in theoretical Marxism, Koestler the Communist sees in History an unfathomable God, overlooks the individual, and is unaware of the permutation of subjective and objective factors which is the key to the great Marxists. But Koestler's case is not rare; scientist and objectivistic deviations are quite frequent. Even if the alternatives of subjectivism and objectivism are resolved in Marx's Marxism, the question still remains whether this is so in communism as a reality and

[19] *Ibid.*, p. 246.

whether the majority of Communists believe in incorporating subjectivity, or whether like Koestler they prefer to deny it in theory and practice. Even the mistakes that Koestler makes in his formulation of the problems leads us to the following questions: Is there in reality any alternative between efficacy and humanity, between historical action and morality? Is it true that we have to choose between being a Commissar—working for men from the outside, treating them as instruments—or being a Yogi—that is, calling men to a completely inward reform? Is it true that revolutionary power negates the individual, his judgment, his intentions, his honor, and even his revolutionary honor? Is it true that in the face of a revolutionary power and a world polarized by the class struggle there are only two possible positions: absolute docility or treason? Is it true, finally, that, in the famous saying of Napoleon, politics is the modern tragedy in which the truth of the individual confronts the demands of the collectivity, as the will of the hero in Greek tragedies confronted a destiny determined by the gods? Claude Morgan wrote that *Darkness at Noon* is the work of a *provocateur,* meaning that Koestler blackens revolutionary action the better to discredit it, and invented his soul-destroying dilemmas arbitrarily. But is Rubashov nothing more than a fictional character and are his problems simply imaginary ones?

II. Bukharin and the Ambiguity of History

THERE WOULD BE no occasion for the question that we are raising if the Moscow Trials had established the charges of sabotage and espionage in the same way a fact is established in a laboratory, or if a series of convergent testimonies, cross-examinations, and documents had made it possible to follow the behavior of the accused month by month and to reveal the plot in the way a crime is reconstructed at the hearings. Whatever there may have been in the way of preliminary investigations, which remain secret, the Soviet tribunal could not have got through the job of trying twenty-one accused persons in the space of eleven days.[1] It rarely involved itself on this level, and when it did (with regard to the Copenhagen episode in Zinoviev's trial, for example), the attempt was not very successful. Only once, in Bukharin's trial, did the proceedings and cross-examinations take a classical turn; this, however, concerned a violent attack planned against

[1] We shall be dealing in particular with the trial of Bukharin which took place from 2nd to 13th March, 1938. It is known that Rubashov has the physical traits of Zinoviev and the moral character of Bukharin.

the revolutionary leadership in 1918 and, as Vishynsky was
careful to point out, these crimes committed more than
twenty years ago were covered by the terms of the law.
With regard to more recent events and the clandestine opposition, those who were in a position to testify found themselves *ipso facto* implicated in the trial: the only competent
witnesses were the accused,[2] and as a consequence their statements never give us information on the brute reality. One
can discern friendships and enmities, the struggle between
partisans involved in twenty years of revolutionary politics,
and occasionally the fear of death and servitude. In the best
cases, these are political acts, or stands adopted on the question
of Stalinist leadership. In a trial of this kind, where in principle all documents are missing, we are left with the things
that were said, and at no time do we have any feeling of
reaching through the words to the facts themselves. Some
of the anecdotes have an air of truth, but they only acquaint
us with the accused's state of mind. The alliances with
major foreign powers, the constitution of a veritable opposition bloc, even the offense itself—all inevitably rest at the
level of hearsay. Guilt in this case is not a matter of a clear
relation between a definite act with specific motives and
specific consequences. It is not the guilt of a criminal, who
is known from the porter's testimony to have been the only
one to have entered the house of the crime between nine
and ten o'clock, and whom the gunsmith testifies bought

[2] Those accused in the trial in progress or reserved for special proceedings, as
Vishynsky said in the Act of Accusation. *The Case of the Anti-Soviet "Bloc of
Rightists and Trotskyites,"* Report of Court Proceedings Heard before the Military
Collegium of the Supreme Court of the U.S.S.R. Moscow, March 2–13, 1938.
Published by the People's Commissariat of Justice of the U.S.S.R., Moscow, 1938.

on the eve of the crime a revolver of the same caliber as the fatal bullet, which the coroner testifies to be the cause of the death. The chain of causes, motives, means, and effects of the opposition's activity is not reconstructed. There are only a few facts in a fog of shifting meanings. In writing this, it is not our intention to be polemical: we are limiting ourselves to the description of what the Moscow Trials could possibly be under the conditions in which they took place— and to the formulation of the impression of a ceremony of language conveyed by the Report of Court Proceedings.

This remark leads us to the heart of the question. For if the trials were only a banal affair of treason paid for by foreigners, the procedure could not have remained so completely clandestine. Anyone who has worked with the Resistance knows that it was far more dangerous to work with paid agents (as the English services often did) than in a political organization. If the opposition's activity left few traces behind, that is because it was a political activity. The accusation can only rely on a few facts because the oppositionist's activities were not strictly acts of treason or sabotage and only fell within the jurisdiction of the constitutional laws of the state through interpretation. The Trials remain on a subjective level and never approach what is called "true" justice, objective and timeless, *because they bear upon facts still open toward the future, which consequently are not yet univocal and only acquire a definitively criminal character when they are viewed from the perspective on the future held by the men in power.*

To put the same thing another way, the Moscow Trials are in the form and style that belong to the Revolution. For

the revolutionary judges what exists in the name of what
does not yet exist, but which he regards as more real. The
act of revolution presents itself both as the creation of history and as the truth of history in relation to its total meaning, and it is essential to the revolution that no one has a
right to ignorance of the law. Bourgeois justice adopts the
past as its precedent; revolutionary justice adopts the future. It
judges in the name of the Truth that the Revolution is about
to make true; its proceedings are part of a *praxis* which
may well be motivated but transcends any particular motive.
That is why it does not concern itself with finding out
whether the accused's motives or intentions were honest
or dishonest; it is only a matter of knowing whether in
effect his conduct, considered from the standpoint of the
collective *praxis,* is revolutionary or not. Thus the smallest
detail acquires an immense significance, the suspect is as
good as guilty, at the same time that the conviction, applying only to the accused's historical role, does not affect his
personal honor, which is in any case considered an abstraction since for the revolutionary we are through and through
what we are for others and in our relations to them.

The Moscow Trials do not create a new legality, since
they apply existing laws to the accused. But they are revolutionary inasmuch as they posit the absolute validity of the
Stalinist perspective on Soviet development, and in evalu-
ating the acts of the opposition they regard as absolutely
objective a view of the future which, though probable, is
subjective, inasmuch as the future does not yet exist for us.
In other terms still, since a revolution presupposes in those

who make it the assurance of understanding what they are living through, the revolutionaries dominate their present the same way historians dominate the past. That is certainly the case with the Moscow Trials: the prosecutor and the accused speak in the name of universal history, as yet unfinished, because they believe they can reach it through the Marxist absolute of action which is indivisibly objective and subjective. The Moscow Trials only make sense between revolutionaries, that is to say between men who are convinced that they are *making history* and who consequently already see the present as past and see those who hesitate as traitors.

More exactly, the Moscow Trials are revolutionary trials presented as if they were ordinary trials. The prosecutor sets himself the specific task of proving that the accused are common law criminals. But at this level there is not even the beginnings of a proof—not a single fact on the sabotage, and, as for the conversations with major foreign powers, just a few discussions over principles among the opposition and . . . an article in a Japanese newspaper. Considered from the standpoint of common law, Bukharin's trial hardly got underway. On the other hand, everything becomes clear if we take it as an historical action. That is what the French Communists admit implicitly. For they have hardly ever insisted on the "proofs" of sabotage and espionage and they have defended the Moscow Trials above all on the level of history. Thus one arrives at the seeming paradox that in the country of the Revolution the opposition's acts are presented as common law crimes, while in France, on the contrary, they are condemned mainly, according to the revolutionary way, as crimes against history.[3] In 1937 Aragon wrote:

> The scandalous advocates of Trotsky and his group should keep quiet. Or else they should know that to make out the innocence of these men is to support the entire Nazi position. If they are doubtful about this little detail or the other, they imply by this very fact . . . that it was not Hitler who burned down the Reichstag, that the *Matin* was right in the Koutrierov affair and the *Jour* in the Navachin affair. They acquit Hitler and the Gestapo in the Spanish rebellion, they deny the Fascist intervention in Spain . . . At best they believe they are now defending men whom they would still like to regard as revolutionaries; in reality, they are defending Hitler and the Gestapo.[4]

If a critical attitude toward the Soviet tribunal is betrayal of the proletariat, with all the more reason is an opposition toward the Soviet government. Rubashov says the very same thing. "To go against Stalin," wrote two Russian authors, "would mean going against collectivization, against the five year plans, against socialism. That would mean joining the camp of the enemies of socialism and the Soviet Union, going over to the Fascist camp."[5]

This puts the discussion on the proper level. It also means recognizing that the Moscow Trials are not an act of time-

---

[3] What happens is that in a country where there has been a revolution which lasted several years and is still going on, there is a resort to established law rather than invoke once more the exigencies of the revolutionary future. On the contrary where there has been no revolution, revolutionary motifs are present in all their novelty. The land of the revolution cannot see itself with the same eyes as the Communists of other countries.

[4] *Commune,* 1937, pp. 804–805.

[5] M. Kline and S. Marchala, *Commune,* 1937, p. 818.

less justice but a phase in the political struggle and an expression of the violence in history. For even if after the event this evaluation of the opposition's historical role appears correct, in view of the outbreak of war, in 1938 it could not have passed for an indisputable truth. At that time it was a subjective view open to error; the Moscow sentences were *not yet* the very judgment of History and they necessarily had an arbitrary look. It is always that way. Even of him whom events will "prove right" it is no accident that we say "he will be right"; for he possesses no science of the future and only has a probable conception of it, so that if he forces others in the name of his vision we rightly speak of violence. As long as there are men, a society, and an open history, such conflicts remain a possibility and our historical or objective responsibility is only our responsibility in the eyes of other men; we may believe we are innocent as we stand before their tribunals, and they may condemn us at the very moment we feel no other blame than that—which all men share—of having judged without absolute certainty. Since, in respect of the future, we have no other criterion than probability, the difference between a greater or lesser probability suffices as the basis of a political decision, but not to leave all the honor on one side and the dishonor on the other.

In the *Cahiers du Bolshevisme* Cogniot only managed to subsume the opposition's acts under the category of penal law by drawing into his definition of "penal" the consequent defense of democracy against fascism:

At the present moment, under today's conditions, what defines the Trotskyite movement is its decidedly criminal character which deserves the reprobation of any consequent democracy in the world, that is to say, any democracy which is determined to combat fascism . . . Whoever protects the accused in the Moscow Trials makes himself the accomplice of every one of the present attacks launched by Fascism against peace and against the workers of the whole world.[6]

When the very existence of popular regimes is in question, the political and the penal are no longer distinguished, as in a besieged village where larceny becomes a crime. So a political error counts as a *faux pas* and opposition becomes treason. In keeping with the revolutionary tradition, such a view questions the abstract distinctions of liberal thought.

In reality, there is not a judicial order *and* a political order, for these are never anything but two expressions of the way the total society operates, so that the liberal ideal of justice plays a role in the operation of conservative societies. Ordinarily, one is simply not aware of the difference. In war and revolution, which are extreme situations where tolerance amounts to weakness, we find a constant overlap between the judicial and the political. Just as formerly the anti-Dreyfus war councils set aside the question of Dreyfus' guilt and considered its consequences first, so Bruhat[7] introduced his defense of the Moscow Trials with a description of the maneuvers of bourgeois governments ready to make use of the opposition. The socialist Sellier entreats the hesitant to listen "where the complaints are coming from and

[6] *Commune*, 1938, pp. 63–64.
[7] *Cahiers du Bolshevisme*, No. 3, March, 1938.

who profits by artificial indignation. Then they would understand immediately"—he adds—"where duty lies."[8] When Georges Friedmann expressed regret that the Central Committee had not "avoided at least in some cases 'the logic of the struggle' that led the opposition to forfeit its rights," Politzer[9] replied that since capitalism and Hitler are behind the opposition, Friedmann in fact regretted that the Central Committee did not make concessions to "Nazi imperialism."

Even today, Claude Morgan deplores that Koestler's book should reopen the question of Moscow Trials after Stalingrad had shown what danger lay in an opposition in time of war. Claude Roy writes that even if it were possible that Rubashov had never been either a traitor or a saboteur, he was a dilettante and was at least guilty of not having understood that his attitude in fact served Hitler. But Rubashov shares the same view. That is the very reason that he gives in. In the end everyone agrees that political acts are to be judged not only according to their meaning for the moral agent but also according to the sense they acquire in the historical context and dialectical phase in which such acts originate. Moreover, it is impossible to see how a Communist could disavow this approach, as it is essential to Marxist thought. In a world of struggle—and for Marxists history is the history of class struggles—there is no margin of indifferent action which classical thought accords to individuals; for every action unfolds and we are responsible for its consequences. Pierre Unik formulates the situation in a quota-

[8] *Ibid.*
[9] *Ibid.*, No. 5–6, May–June, 1938, pp. 184–185.

tion from Saint-Just: "A patriot is one who supports the
Republic as a whole; whoever resists it in detail is a traitor."[10]
Either this means nothing at all, or else it means that in a
period of revolutionary tension or external threat there is no
clear-cut boundary between political divergences and objective treason. Humanism is suspended and government is
Terror.

At this point people become indignant and cry out against
barbarism. In reality the most serious threat to civilization is
not to kill a man because of his ideas (this has often been
done in wartime), but to do so without recognizing it or
saying so, and to hide revolutionary justice behind the mask
of the penal code. For, by hiding violence one grows accus-
tomed to it and makes an institution of it. On the other
hand, if one gives violence its name and if one uses it, as the
revolutionaries always did, without pleasure, there remains
a chance of driving it out of history. In any case violence will
not be expelled by locking ourselves within the judicial dream
of liberalism. Today a decadent liberalism and rationalism
use an amazing method of criticism which consists in making ideologies responsible for the situations which they describe at the outset—existentialism is blamed for contingency
and communism for violence. The maxim of the Moscow
Trials according to which opposition is treason has its coun-
terpart and justification in Franco's fifth column. It may be
objected that here fascism has learned the lesson of Bolshevism. But this "who started it?" is puerile. The development of communism is not an absolutely new departure; it
expresses the aggravation of the social struggle and the de-

[10] *Commune*, 1938, *ibid*.

composition of the liberal world as much as being the cause of these phenomena, and if it precipitates them it is because historical restorations are impossible and violence can only be transcended in the violent creation of a new order.

In 1939 we were still living under the liberal order. We had not yet come to understand that the "legitimate diversity of opinion" always presupposes a fundamental agreement and is only possible on the basis of what is uncontested. Albert Sarrault really marked the limits of liberalism when he exclaimed in the chamber, "Communism is not a viewpoint, it is a crime!" That was the moment for us to have seen the dogmatic basis of liberalism and the way it only grants certain liberties by taking away the freedom to choose against it.[11] But such uses of the franchise were not usual among liberals. In daily politics they professed, verbally at least, to have "no enemies on the left," and tried to avoid the problem of revolution. Thus we conducted our politics in the conviction (all the stronger for not being articulated) that the vicissitudes of history can be weathered through respect for opinion and that though divided over means, we

[11] Here we are not speaking in favor of an anarchical liberty: if I wish freedom for another person it is inevitable that even this wish will be seen by him as an alien law; and so liberalism turns into violence. One can only blind oneself to this outcome by refusing to reflect upon the relation between the self and others. The anarchist who closes his eyes to this dialectic is nonetheless exposed to its consequences. It is the basic fact on which we have to build freedom. We are not accusing liberalism of being a system of violence; we reproach it with not seeing its own face in violence, with veiling the pact upon which it rests while rejecting as barbarous that other source of freedom—revolutionary freedom—which is the origin of all social pacts. With the assumptions of impersonal Reason and rational Man, and by regarding itself as a natural rather than an historical fact, liberalism assumes universality as a datum whereas the problem is its realization through the dialectic of concrete intersubjectivity.

are basically agreed upon ends so that a concordance of wills is possible.

This is what Marxists deny. The Marxist revolution is not irrational because it is the extrapolation and conclusion of the logic of the present. However, the latter, according to Marxism, is only fully perceptible in a certain social situation and for the proletarians who are the only ones to live the revolution because they are the only ones who experience oppression. For the others revolution may be a duty or a concept but they can only live it by proxy, and insofar as they rejoin the proletariat. Even when they do this, the ideas and motifs cannot and need not be determining, for then their collaboration would be conditional. Everything depends on a fundamental decision not just to understand the world but to change it, and to join up with those who are changing the world as a spontaneous development in their own lives. The critique of the subject reflecting in terms of generalities, the resort to the proletariat as the agency which is not only revolutionary in thought but in action as well, the idea that the revolution is not just an affair of reason and will, but a matter of existence, or that "universal" reason is class reason and that inversely proletarian *praxis* is the vehicle of an effective universality—in a word, the least element of Marxism shows (in the sense the word has in chemistry) man's creative force in history and reveals the contingency of the liberal pact which is nothing but an historical product whereas it pretends to enunciate an immutable truth of Human Nature.

Since 1939 we have, of course, not lived through any Marxist revolution but we have been through a war and an occupation, the two experiences being comparable in that both involve *questioning what can be taken for granted.* In the political life of France the defeat of 1940 was an event unequalled by the greatest dangers of 1914–1918. For many men it had the value of a radical doubt and a revolutionary significance because it laid bare the contingency of the foundations of legality and showed how one constructs a new legality. For the first time in a long while, one could witness the dissociation of formal legality and moral authority; the state apparatus lost its legitimacy and its sacred character in favor of a state yet to be built and existing only in the will of men. For the first time in ages every officer and official, instead of living in the shadow of an established state, found himself invited to question himself on the nature of the social pact and to reconstitute the state through his choice. Here simple reason was not enough: whether one understood it as a calculation of chance or as a universal moral rule, it provided us with no conclusion, since it was necessary to choose without reservation and to choose against other men, since conscience found itself pushed back into the dogmatisms of struggle to the death. In this way the passional and illegal origins of all legality and reason emerged. No longer was there any "legitimate diversity of opinions." Men condemned one another to death as traitors because they did not see the future in the same way. Intentions no longer counted, only actions. It is well known that many grown men, or young men ill-suited to radical responsibilities, proved beneath the test. Overcome by dizziness they looked to the formal legality of the Vichy regime for a point of stability, which they hoped for in de Gaulle's government, once it was recognized. It is also known how many of the liberals dropped as soon as possible, along with their revolutionary uniform, the responsibilities of creation, and that as soon as de Gaulle's government was established it sought every means of forgetting its own origins in insurrection and managed it quite well. But what had to be done in the purges still arouses the memory of a time when the state was suspended, its decisions and laws made null, when reason was violence and liberty unrespected.

For it is a fact that the death sentences were voted on even when the cross-examinations, as in the case of Laval, were shortened—and the sentences would have been voted even if there had been no cross-examination. Once peace is restored, the government and magistrates are loath to admit that one can be condemned because of his ideas, and that is why the prosecution almost always tries to uncover a malicious intent. We experience a kind of relief when it can be shown that the accused's political passions led him to plot against his country and against liberty, or that he wanted power, glory, money. But even if, as happens, the prosecution fails on both scores, it is enough for one victim of the collaboration to step forth to testify and the sentence is a certainty. It is quite unlikely that Pétain deliberately sought to ruin the French army in order to satisfy his reactionary interests. The hypothesized plot, which is always ventured by prosecutors because they share the police chief's naive idea of history made by individual machinations, was no more successful in the trial of Pétain than in the Moscow Trials. It is possible that neither Pétain nor Laval one day decided to sell themselves to Germany, or to keep power, or even to see a certain policy prevail. And yet, even if there was no fault in this sense we would not absolve them as men who simply made a mistake. Even if it were established that they had no other motive than their country's interests, even if it were not premature to have considered a German victory certain at a point where, as de Gaulle said, there were still considerable reserve forces in the world which could still alter the outcome of the war, even if there were not something suspect in the speed with which they registered the result, even if in all probability Germany in 1940 was on the eve of a certain victory, their decision to collaborate would not appear any less criminal.

Are we saying that the German occupation should have been met with an heroic refusal beyond all hope? A pure morality "without any exception"? Such a refusal, the decision not only to risk death but to die rather than live under foreign domination or fascism is, like suicide, an absolutely gratuitous act, which is beyond existence. Though possible through me and for me, it loses its meaning when imposed externally and by government decision. It is an individual attitude, it is not a political position. What is meant by the condemnation of the collaborators' choice is that no actual situation in history is absolutely compelling, and the proposition "Germany will probably win the war" could not in 1940 be a simple assertion, but brought to a still uncertain event, an irrevocable seal; it means that in history there is no absolute neutrality or objectivity, that the apparent innocent judgment which states a probability in reality sketches what is possible, and that every existential judgment is a value judgment; even *laisser faire* involves a commitment.

But with respect to the events of 1940, how do we know all this? Through the fact of the allied victory. It shows peremptorily that the collaboration was not necessary, that it involved initiative, and despite what it might have been or thought it was, the collaboration is thereby transformed into a voluntary betrayal. There is a sort of maleficence in history: it solicits men, tempts them so that they believe they are moving in its direction, and then suddenly it unmasks, and events change and prove that there was another possibility. The men whom history abandons in this way and who see themselves simply as accomplices suddenly find themselves the instigators of a crime to which history has inspired them. And *they are unable to look for excuses or to excuse themselves from even a part of the responsibility*. For at the very moment when they were following the apparent curve of history, others were deciding to back off and to commit their lives along another road to the future. Thus it was not completely beyond human powers. Were they madmen? Did they win by luck? And does one have the right to accord the same compassion to those shot in the Occupation as to those shot in the purges who were just as much victims of historical fortune? Or were these men who read history better, who set aside their passions and acted in response to the truth?

But what we reproach the collaborators for is surely not a mistake in reading any more than what we honor in the Resistance is simply coolness of judgment and clairvoyance. On the contrary, what one admires is that they took sides against the probable and that they were devoted and enthusiastic enough to allow reasons to speak to them that only came afterward. The glory of those who resisted—like the dishonor of the collaborators—presupposes both the contingency of history, without which no one would be to blame in politics, and the rationality of history, without which there would be only madmen. Those who resisted were neither madmen nor wise men; they were heroes— men in whom passion and reason were identical, who in the obscurity of desire did what history expected and what was later to appear as the truth of the moment. We cannot remove the element of reason in their choice any more than the element of audacity and risk of failure.

By confronting the collaborator before he was in the wrong historically, and him who resisted before history proved him right, and both again after history had shown the one wrong and the other right, the Moscow Trials reveal the subjective struggle to the death which characterizes contemporary history. In the course of collaborating, the accused, who had not believed what he was doing involved dishonorable conduct, was representing Gaullism in London and collaboration in Paris as the two main French interests in face of the uncertainty of history. What was odious about the argument was that it justified Gaullists and collaborationists alike—as if the question were one of speculative hypotheses, whereas in fact it was necessary to be one *or* the other and each sought the death of the other. On the historical level, being a collaborator was not just a matter of occupying one of the two attitudes open to Frenchmen but asserting that there was only one view and to side with the militia and the execution of members of the Resistance. We could only exercise impartiality and justify everyone in re-

gard to a past which had completely evolved (if ever there
was such a thing).

With respect to the recent past, the person who judges
takes up a definite position exclusive of all others and he
either wins or loses with what he has chosen. The disgust
former collaborators feel for the purges simply proves that
they never tried to imagine the lot of those whose death they
demanded. To ask that the juries in the purges furnish
"guarantees of impartiality" proves that those involved have
never taken sides absolutely, for if they had done so they
would know that when it is radical, an historical decision is
both partial and absolute, that it can only be judged by
another decision, and finally that only the Resistance had
the right to punish or forgive the collaborators. It is shameful that the same magistrates who summoned the Communists summon the collaborators today in the name of the
state and the established law. Here it is impartiality that is
dishonorable and partiality which is just. Even the idea of
an objective justice in this case has no sense since it would
have to compare mutually exclusive actions between which
reason alone is not enough to decide.

The purges resume and concentrate the paradox of history which is that a contingent future, once it enters the
present, appears real and even necessary. There appears here
a harsh notion of responsibility, based not on what men intended but what they find they have achieved in the light of
the event. No one can protest it; a member of the Resistance
projected onto 1940 and the beginnings of Gaullism the outcome of 1944 and the Gaullist victory; he judged the past in
the name of the present. But in order to reject collaboration

he did not wait for Gaullism to come into power, but rejected collaboration in the name of the future he was seeking. On his side, the collaborator fashioned a destiny out of a provisional situation and extrapolated a momentary present into the future. On both sides, an absolute choice of relative considerations was involved, a choice sanctioned by deaths. Any "impartial" arbitrator between these choices is disqualified by this very fact, any "impersonal" justice is thereby illegitimate. These things happen due to the absolute exigencies of political choice which the liberals ignore. Good or bad, innocent or guilty, brave or cowardly, to the Resistance the collaborator is a traitor and thus a traitor objectively or historically the day the Resistance is victorious.

Historical responsibility transcends the categories of liberal thought—intention and act, circumstances and will, objective and subjective. It overwhelms the individual in his acts, mingles the objective and subjective, imputes circumstances to the will; thus it substitutes for the individual as he feels himself to be a role or phantom in which he cannot recognize himself, but in which he must see himself, since that is what he was for his victims. And today it is his victims who are right.

The war experience may help us to understand the dilemmas of Rubashov and the Moscow Trials. To be sure, there was no Montoire interview between Hitler and Bukharin; when Bukharin was tried the enemy was no longer or not yet on Soviet soil. But in a country which since 1917 had known only extreme situations, even before the war and the invasion, opposition could well look like treason. Whatever the opposition may have wanted and even if it was a more certain future for the Revolution, it remains that in fact it weakened the U.S.S.R. In any case, by one of those sudden reversals so frequent in history, the events of 1941 accuse them of treason. Like the trials of the disinterested collaborators, the Moscow Trials might be seen as the drama of subjective honesty and objective treason. There would only be two differences. The first is that the convictions in the purges cannot bring those who died back to life, whereas suppression could save the U.S.S.R. losses and defeats. The Moscow Trials would thus be more cruel, since they anticipate the judgment of events, and less cruel since they contribute to a coming victory. The other difference is that the Marxist defendants, in this case being in agreement over the principle of historical responsibility, became their own prosecutors; to discover their subjective honesty we have looked through their own declarations as well as the summons.

Such is the hypothesis which one is led to if one proceeds, in accordance with strict Marxist method, from historical circumstances to the Trials themselves, from what it was possible for them to be to what in fact they were. It remains to show that this method, and it alone, makes it possible to understand the proceedings in detail. It ought to reveal, unless we are mistaken, the two senses possessed by the same facts, depending on whether they are viewed from the perspective of the future or some other viewpoint, and how the two senses fuse with one another so that opposition is treason and treason is merely opposition.

The ambiguity is visible from the very beginning. On one side, at the opening of the proceedings, Bukharin pleads "guilty to the charges brought against me"[12] and which have just been enumerated by the prosecution. It involves his participation, at times direct, at others indirect, in a "conspiratorial group named the 'bloc of Rightists and Trotskyites' . . . with the object of espionage on behalf of foreign states, wrecking, diversionist and terrorist activities, undermining the military power of the U.S.S.R., working for the defeat of the U.S.S.R., dismembering the U.S.S.R., . . . lastly with the object of overthrowing the Socialist social and state system existing in the U.S.S.R. and of restoring capitalism and the power of the bourgeoisie in the U.S.S.R.,"[13] as well as "a number of terrorist acts against leaders of the C.P.S.U. and the Soviet government."[14] Bukharin admits personal responsibility for all the acts of the "bloc of Rightists and Trotskyites."[15] He considers himself already condemned to death.[16] And yet he refuses to regard himself as a spy, traitor, saboteur, and terrorist. He gave no orders for sabotage (p. 770). After Brest Litovsk he did not arrange the assassination of Lenin but only a reversal of the Party line and Lenin's arrest for twenty-four hours (p. 448). This

---

[12] *Report of Court Proceedings,* p. 36.

[13] *Ibid.,* p. 34. Definition of the Charge.

[14] *Ibid.*

[15] "Consequently, I plead guilty to what directly follows from this, the sum total of crimes committed by this counter-revolutionary organization, irrespective of whether or not I knew of, whether or not I took a direct part in any particular act. Because I am responsible as one of the leaders and not as a cog of this counter-revolutionary organization" (p. 370).

[16] "I have merited the most severe punishment, and I agree with Citizen the Procurator, who several times repeated that I stand on the threshold of the hour of my death" (p. 768). "The severest sentence would be justified, because a man deserves to be shot ten times over for such crimes" (p. 775).

project, which Bukharin had first spoken of in an article of
1934, could well appear criminal in 1938, by which time
Lenin had become an historical figure and the dictatorship
had hardened. In the atmosphere of 1918 it was not a conspiracy (pp. 474, 490, 507). On five occasions Bukharin categorically denies the charge of espionage (pp. 383, 413, 417,
424, 770) and only Sharangovich and Ivanov were brought
as witnesses against him, themselves charged in the same
trial and treated by him as provocateurs without a word of
protest from the prosecutor Vyshinsky (p. 383). How can
he at once declare himself responsible for acts of treason and
yet reject the name of traitor?

Can one believe in the confessions without believing in
the denials? Each is juxtaposed, especially in the final dec-
laration. Can one believe in the denials and refuse all
credence to the confessions? Yet, after the judgments in the
first two trials, how could Bukharin have hoped to save his
life by confessing? If it had been forced on him by physical
or moral torture, one would not see it as incomplete. There
remain the fantastic hypotheses of the journalists. Bukharin
forestalls them, however, and rejects them in his last plea.

> Repentance is often attributed to diverse and absolutely ab-
> surd things like Tibetan powders and the like. I must say of
> myself that in prison, where I was confined for over a year,
> I worked, studied, and retained my clarity of mind . . .
> Hypnotism is suggested. But I conducted my own defence
> in Court from the legal standpoint too, oriented myself on the
> spot, argued with the State Prosecutor; and nobody, even a
> man who has little experience in this branch of medicine, must
> admit that hypnotism of this kind is altogether impossible.

This repentance is often attributed to the Dostoyevsky mind, to the specific properties of the soul (*"l'âme slave"* as it is called), and this can be said of types like Alyosha Karamozov, the heroes of *The Idiot* and other Dostoyevsky characters, who are prepared to stand up in the public square and cry: "Beat me, Orthodox Christians, I am a villain!"

But that is not the case here at all. *"L'âme slave"* and the psychology of Dostoyevsky characters are a thing of the remote past in our country, the pluperfect tense. Such types do not exist in our country, or exist perhaps only on the outskirts of small provincial towns, if they do even there.[17]

Throughout the proceedings as well as in his last plea, Bukharin never looks like a *broken* man. As we have seen, he is not a guilty man trying to avoid the truth, but neither is he a terrorized innocent. We have the impression of a man in his senses about to carry out a precise and difficult undertaking.

What sort of undertaking? Bukharin set out to show that his acts of opposition, which were based on a certain appraisal of the course of the Revolution in the U.S.S.R. and the rest of the world, could be used either inside or outside the U.S.S.R. by all the opponents of collectivization. His acts having provided them with an ideological platform thereby assumed counterrevolutionary proportions, although he himself, of course, had never been in the service of a foreign power. But he was not able to say all that; to say it in so many words would have been to separate personal integrity and historical responsibility and ultimately to reject the judgment of history. But between Bukharin and the court,

[17] *Ibid.*, p. 777.

while there was no express agreement, there was at least the tacit bond that both were Marxists. Bukharin was therefore able only to introduce nuances, to argue and to clarify. The only weapon he allowed himself was irony. For the rest, if they condemned him, he would not object. Our task at the moment is to say what he was able only to suggest.

At the source of the "crimes" there are only the conversation between the opponents of forced collectivization and the authoritarian leadership of the Party. Collectivization was begun prematurely. Socialism is not possible in a single country. In Russia the Revolution preceded economic development with the result that Russian politics necessarily has a strictly national character and the movement of world revolution can only be oriented in terms of the basic needs of the Soviet Union. World capitalism is in a state of stabilization rather than revolutionary contagion as hoped for by the men of 1917. It is useless to go against the tide of events and impossible to force history, and thus the New Economic Policy must be pushed more extensively. Such a policy is not in itself counterrevolutionary. In 1922 Lenin, who was not afraid of words, defended NEP as a policy of "retreat" along the line of "State capitalism." And he added:

It seems very strange to everyone that a non-socialist element should be rated higher than, regarded superior to, socialism in a republic which declares itself a socialist republic. But the fact will become intelligible if you recall that we definitely did not regard the economic system of Russia as something homogeneous and highly developed; we were fully aware that in Russia we had a patriarchal agriculture, i.e., the most primitive form of agriculture, alongside the socialist form . . . in 1921, after we had passed through the most important stage of the Civil War—and passed through it victoriously—we felt the impact of a grave—I think it was the gravest—internal political crisis in Soviet Russia. This internal crisis brought to light discontent not only among a considerable section of the peasantry but also among the workers. This was the first and, I hope, the last time in the history of Soviet Russia that feeling ran against us among large masses of the peasants, not consciously but instinctively. What gave rise to this peculiar, and for us, of course, very unpleasant, situation? The reason for it was that in our economic offensive we had run too far ahead, that we had not provided ourselves with adequate resources, that the masses sensed what we ourselves were not then able to formulate consciously but what we admitted soon after, a few weeks later, namely, that the direct transition to purely socialist forms, to purely socialist distribution, was beyond our available strength, and that if we were unable to effect a retreat so as to confine ourselves to easier tasks, we would face disaster. The crisis began, I think, in February 1921. In the spring of that year we decided unanimously—I did not observe any considerable disagreement among us on this question—to adopt the New Economic Policy.[18]

After the experience of NEP—and moreover in conformity with the views of the left opposition—the Party found it indispensable to put an end to the concessions. It turned to the offensive on all fronts. The forced collectivization was begun and it was then in an atmosphere of civil war that

[18] V. I. Lenin, "Five Years of the Russian Revolution and the Prospects of the World Revolution," *Report to the Fourth Congress of the Communist International*, November 13, 1922, *Collected Works*, Vol. 33, pp. 419 and 421–422.

Bukharin and "his friends upheld the attitudes of NEP." I consider this stage the transition to "double entry bookkeeping all along the line."[19] This means that once the Stalinist leadership had embarked on a thorough collectivization, the opposition found themselves willy-nilly in the role of counterrevolutionaries. One needs to know that their language was rough. Ryutin's platform of which Bukharin is said to have had knowledge, called Stalin the "great *agent provocateur*" and "the gravedigger of the Revolution and the Party." This being the case, why should Bukharin not be a *provocateur,* in the language of the Stalinists? Trotsky supported a program of industrialization, but by more gentle methods. In the face of the forced collectivization, Trotsky was in fact on the side of the kulak, says Bukharin: "Trotsky had to throw off his Leftist uniform. When it came to exact formulations of what had to be done after all, his Right platform came into evidence at once, that is, he had to speak of decollectivization, etc."[20] The violent policy of the Stalinist leadership had created a crisis in which only two parties were possible: to be for or to be against, so that any discussion about means involved a separation between collectivization and industrialization. Did we *intend* to restore capitalism is what Bukharin asks in effect. That is not the question. It is not a matter of what we had in mind but of what we were actually doing.

I want to speak of another aspect of the matter, from a more important standpoint, *from the objective side of this matter, because here there arises the problem of accountability and*

[19] *Report of the Court Proceedings,* p. 387.
[20] *Ibid.,* p. 389.

judgment from the standpoint of the crimes revealed in Court . . .

The Right counter-revolutionaries seemed at first to be a "deviation"; they seemed, at first glance, to be people who began with discontent in connection with collectivization, in connection with industrialization, with the fact, as they claimed, that industrialization was destroying production. This, at first glance, seemed to be the chief thing. . . . When all the state machines, when all the means, when all the best forces were flung into the industrialization of the country, into collectivization, we found ourselves, literally in twenty-four hours, on the other shore, we found ourselves with the kulaks, with the counter-revolutionaries, we found ourselves with the capitalist remnants which still existed at the time in the sphere of trade. . . . We, the counter-revolutionary plotters, came at that time more and more to display the psychology that collective farms were music of the future. What was necessary was to develop rich property owners. This was the tremendous change that took place in our standpoint and psychology. . . . In 1917 it would never have occurred to any of the members of the Party, myself included, to pity Whiteguards who had been killed; yet in the period of the liquidation of the kulaks, in 1929–30, we pitied the expropriated kulaks. . . . To whom would it have occurred in 1919 to blame the dislocation of our economic life on the Bolsheviks and not on sabotage? To nobody. It would have sounded as frank and open treason. Yet I myself in 1928 invented the formula about the military-feudal exploitation of the peasantry, that is, I put the blame for the costs of the class struggle not on the class which was hostile to the proletariat, but on the leaders of the proletariat itself. This was already a swing of 180 degrees. This meant that ideological and political platforms grew into counter-revolu-

tionary platforms. . . . The logic of the struggle led to the
logic of ideas and to a change of our psychology, to the
counter-revolutionizing of our aims.[21]

On each of the main charges, Bukharin's viewpoint is the
same: he traces the origins of his activity to a certain evaluation of the outlook and shows that in the situation given
and in the logic of the struggle his evaluation was in fact
counterrevolutionary, and he is therefore guilty of historical
treason. It is quite evident that Bukharin was no Fascist. He
even took precautions against the Bonapartist tendencies
that he suspected in military circles. What is true is that in
the battle over collectivization, the opposition could only
rely on the kulaks, Mensheviks, and the remaining elements
of revolutionary socialists—could only overthrow the Party
leadership with their help—that it would have to share
power with them and that thus in the end there were "elements of Caesarism"[22] involved. No, it is quite obvious that
Bukharin was not linked with White Guard emigré Cossack
circles. But politically he was interested in the kulak opposition. He kept informed on the kulak revolts through friends
coming from the northern Caucasus or from Siberia, who in
turn got their information from Cossack circles. Consequently, he accepts responsibility for these revolts.[23]

Marxist politics is not primarily a system of ideas but a
reading of ongoing history; and as a Marxist Bukharin was

[21] *Ibid.,* pp. 380–381. Author's emphasis. It is clear that here Bukharin is
saying what he thinks and is giving his own version of the opposition's "crimes,"
as is confirmed by the President's intervention (". . . you are giving us a
lecture," p. 381).

[22] *Ibid.,* p. 382.

[23] *Ibid.,* p. 400.

not trying so much to set on foot a *plan* as to discover what he believed to be the forces on the move inside the U.S.S.R. In this spirit he stated that "the North Caucasus was one of the places where discontent among the peasantry was manifesting itself and will manifest itself most vividly."[24] If after that one "dots the 'i's," as he says, and changes an attempt to complicity, there occurs an enlargement and falsification of the facts, although their interpretation remains historically permissible because political man is defined not by what he himself does but by the forces on which he counts. The prosecutor's role is to reveal Bukharin's activity on the plane of history and objectivity. Bukharin regards the interpretation as legitimate; he only wants it to be known that it is an interpretation and that it is only from a certain standpoint that he was linked with the Cossacks.

> VYSHINSKY: Accused Bukharin, is it a fact or not that a group of your confederates in the North Caucasus was connected with Whiteguard emigré Cossack circles abroad? Is that a fact or not? Rykov says it is . . .
>
> BUKHARIN: If Rykov says it is I have no grounds for not believing him . . .
>
> VYSHINSKY: Answer me "No."
>
> BUKHARIN: I cannot say "No," and I cannot deny that it did take place.
>
> VYSHINSKY: So the answer is neither "Yes" or "No"? . . .
>
> BUKHARIN: From the point of view of mathematical probability it can be said, with very great probability, that is a fact.[25]

Vyshinsky takes his stand in a world of objects where noth-

24 *Ibid.*, p. 136.
25 *Ibid.*, pp. 400–401 (Translator).

ing is indeterminate. He would like to erase the region of indeterminism, Bukharin's conscience, where there exist *things not yet known,* empty zones; he would like to leave only *things he has made or had made.*

A consistent opposition cannot ignore the foreigner pressing against the frontiers of the U.S.S.R.: "Advantage should be taken of the antagonisms between the imperialist powers,"[26] in other words, to side with certain bourgeois states against others and at least "neutralize"[27] the other side. At Brest Litovsk the Soviet government had neutralized Germany at the price of partial dismemberment, and the opposition, since it believes itself to be in accordance with the sense of history, evidently has the same rights. It also has the same responsibilities: to form an indirect alliance with the enemy is already to aid him. In such probing, it is obvious that each side tries to outwit the other. A rather unreliable method, remarks Vyshinsky. "That always happens,"[28] Bukharin replies. And indeed in a world where, apart from past contracts, the power of each party to a contract remains a tacit clause, every pact signifies something else than what is stipulated in it; a diplomatic overture is a sign of weakness and is always a risky step, as in this particular case where the risk is that Bukharin might be reproached with the neutralization of Germany as an act of treason whereas for the 1917 government (which moreover did not have the choice) it is a glorious act. For his own part Bukharin was opposed to the territorial concessions, but he had to reckon with

26 *Ibid.,* p. 770.
27 *Ibid.,* p. 408, 422.
28 *Ibid.,* p. 437.

those of his friends who thought them necessary at the time. Of course, the concessions were not specified and the opposition did not sell the Ukraine to gain power. But some of the opposition members believed it would come to that.

Everything lies in this appraisal of certain eventualities as already achieved. For his part Bukharin was not a defeatist. But many in the opposition thought the U.S.S.R. incapable of resisting foreign aggression on her own.[29] If one considers defeat inevitable, it has to be assumed as a given in the problem. Every action presupposes a calculation of the future which enters into its inevitability. Even if we assume that there is, strictly speaking, a science of the past, no one has ever held that there was a science of the future, and Marxists are the last ones to do so. There are *perspectives,* but, as the word implies, this involves only a horizon of probabilities, comparable to our perceptual horizon which can, as we approach it and it becomes present to us, reveal itself to be quite different from what we were expecting. Only the major features are certain, or, more exactly, certain possibilities are excluded: for example, a definite stabilization of capitalism is excluded. But how and by what paths socialism will become a reality is left to a conjecture of events whose difficulty Lenin emphasized when he said that progress is not straight like the Nevsky Prospect. This means not only that delays may be necessary but that we do not even *know* when starting an offensive whether it ought to be pursued to the limit, or if instead it is necessary to switch to a strategic retreat. This can only be decided in the course

---

[29] It is well known that Trotsky formulated this prognosis quite categorically in *The Revolution Betrayed,* New York, Doubleday, Doran, 1937.

of the struggle and with an eye to the adversary's behavior.[30] Every outline of the possibilities, even if it is justified by a great number of facts, is nevertheless a choice and expresses, along with certain objective possibilities, the strength and justice of the revolutionary consciousness in every individual. *He who outlines an offensive can always be treated as a provocateur and he who outlines a retreat can always be treated as a counterrevolutionary.* Bukharin's friends reckoned on defeat and acted accordingly. But to reckon *with* is, in a certain way, to reckon *on*.

The entire polemic between Vyshinsky and Bukharin turns up these two tiny words.

BUKHARIN: When I asked Tomsky how he conceived the mechanics of the coup he said this was the business of the military organization, which was to open the front.

VYSHINSKY: So Tomsky was preparing to open the front?

BUKHARIN: He did not say that. . . . He said "was to" ("dolzhna"); but the meaning of these words is *"müssen"* and not *"sollen."*

---

[30] "We must not only know how to act when we pass directly to the offensive and are victorious. In revolutionary times this is not so difficult, nor so very important; at least it is not the most decisive thing. There are always times in a revolution when the opponent loses his head; and if we attack him at such a time we may win an easy victory. But that is nothing, because our enemy, if he has enough endurance, can rally his forces beforehand, and so forth. He can easily provoke us to attack him and then throw us back for many years. For this reason, I think, the idea that we must prepare for ourselves the possibility of retreat is very important, and not only from the theoretical point of view. From the practical point of view, too, all the parties which are preparing to take the direct offensive against capitalism in the near future must now give thought to the problem of preparing for a possible retreat." *Report to the Fourth Congress of the Communist International, loc. cit.,* p. 421.

VYSHINSKY: Leave your philosophy aside. In Russian "was to" means "was to."

BUKHARIN: It means that the military circles had the idea that in that case these military circles . . .

VYSHINSKY: No, not the idea, but they were to. That means . . .

BUKHARIN: No, it does not mean.

VYSHINSKY: So they were not to open the front?

BUKHARIN: From whose point of view? Tomsky told me what the military said, what Lenukidze said.

VYSHINSKY: Permit me to read Bukharin's testimony, Vol. V, pp. 95–96 . . . what is written later is: "Whereupon I said that in that case it would be expedient to try those guilty of the defeat at the front. This will enable us to win over the masses by playing on patriotic slogans."

BUKHARIN: The word "play" here was not meant in an odious sense.

VYSHINSKY: Accused Bukharin, that you have here employed a jesuitical method, a perfidious method, is borne out by the following. Permit me to read further: "I had in mind that by this, that is, by the conviction of those guilty of the defeat, we would be able at the same time to rid ourselves of the Bonapartist danger that alarmed me."[31]

The scenario is uncomplicated; there is the patriotism of the masses and among certain of the military there is the spirit of defeatism; the dictatorship will be smashed by defeat and the military will be destroyed with the help of the masses. Bukharin's aim is not patriotic but neither is it antipatriotic. It is a matter of making one of the conjecture of

[31] *Report of Court Proceedings*, pp. 434–436.

events in order to redirect the Party line. Bukharin is not the one who created the defeatism among the military. "Citizen Procurator, I say that was a political fact."[32] History is not a series of plots and machinations in which the course of events is steered by the will of determined individuals. In reality, the conspiracies are synchronizations of existing forces.[33] Political man would be wrong to decline responsibility for the movements he makes use of, just as it would be wrong to impute to him their detailed direction. The philosophy of history might well be enriched by the vocabulary of communism. Communist politics do not choose their ends, they *orient themselves around* forces already at work. They are defined less by their ideas than by the position they occupy in the movement of history. A movement's responsibility is determined by the role it plays in a network of events, just as a man's character resides much more in his basic enterprise than in his explicit choices. Thus it is possible to have to answer for acts of treason without having intended them. A dozen times in the course of the 1938 trials, when pressed the accused answered: "Such was the formula,"[34] "Yes, it can be put that way."[35] "I am in no way better than a spy,"[36] "at that time it was possible to formulate it in this way."[37] To a hasty reader this is the equivalent

[32] *Ibid.*, p. 407.

[33] BUKHARIN: Excuse me, Citizen Procurator, but you are putting the question in a very personal way. This trend arose . . .

VYSHINSKY: I am not asking when this trend arose, I am asking when this group was organized (p. 507).

[34] *Ibid.*, p. 403, Rykov.

[35] *Ibid.*, p. 137, Bukharin.

[36] *Ibid.*, p. 413, Rykov.

[37] *Ibid.*, p. 137, Bukharin.

of a confession (but what difference does it make to be taken as a spy by people who are in a hurry?) To Marxists of the future, these formulas preserve the defendants' revolutionary honor. It is possible that there were negotiations between the opposition and the German government. Did Bukharin know about them? No, but "in general" he considered negotiations useful. Once he knew about them did he approve or disapprove of them? He did not disapprove, therefore he approved.

> VYSHINSKY: I ask you, did you endorse them, or not?
>
> BUKHARIN: I repeat, Citizen Procurator; since I did not disavow them, I consequently endorsed them.
>
> VYSHINSKY: Consequently, you endorsed them?
>
> BUKHARIN: If I did not disavow them, consequently I endorsed them.
>
> VYSHINSKY: That is what I am asking you. That is to say you endorsed them?
>
> BUKHARIN: So then "Consequently" is the same as "that is to say."
>
> VYSHINSKY: What do you mean, "that is to say"?
>
> BUKHARIN: That is to say, I endorsed them.[38]

And Rykov, to finish, gives the reply:

> RYKOV: We are neither of us little children. If you don't endorse such things, then you must fight against them. One cannot play with neutrality in such things.[39]

Only children imagine that their lives are separable from the lives of others, that their responsibility is limited to what they themselves have done, and that there is a boundary be-

38 *Ibid.,* p. 407.
39 *Ibid.,* p. 408.

tween good and evil. A Marxist knows very well that every human undertaking polarizes interests not all of which can be answered for. He simply tries to act in such a way that in all this confusion the forces of progress might prevail. In a world of struggle no one can flatter himself that he has clean hands. Bukharin did not deny the contacts made with the Germans. Stalin signed the Russo-German pact. What does that matter when the question was to save the Revolution, that is to say the future of humanity? Every Marxist (and probably others) is quite familiar with this ambiguity of a history in wounds. That is why their polemics are so violent, why "traitor" and "provocateur" are classical terms in their discussions, why, too, after the fiercest polemics they can be found reconciled. It is because it is not a question of a judgment on the person but the appraisal of an historical role. That is the reason why in the Trials themselves the accused speak man to man with their judges and sometimes seem to be less their adversaries than their collaborators.

But if the opposition was running the risk of counterrevolution, and if it knew this, why did it persist in this tactic? And if it persisted in it, why, on the day of the Trials, did it abandon this line? It is because new facts intervened which completely overthrew their position and transformed opposition into recklessness. The threat of a foreign war became clear.

RAKOVSKY: . . . I remember, and will never forget as long as I live, the circumstances which finally impelled me to give evidence. During one of the examinations, this was in the summer, I learnt, in the first place, that Japanese aggression had begun against China, against the Chinese people, I learnt of

Germany's and Italy's undisguised aggression against the Spanish people . . .

I learnt of the feverish preparations which all the fascist states were making to unleash a world war. What a reader usually absorbs every day in small doses in telegrams, I received once in a big dose. This had a stunning effect on me.[40]

And:

BUKHARIN: I have been in prison for over a year, and therefore do not know what is going on in the world. But, judging from those fragments of real life that sometimes reached me by chance, I see, feel and understand that the interests which we so criminally betrayed are entering a new phase of gigantic development, are now appearing in the international arena as a great and mighty factor of the international proletarian phase.[41]

Forced collectivization and the pace of industrialization or of the Five-Year Plans ceased to be a subject for discussion from the moment it became clear that time was short and that the existence of the Soviet state was at stake. The threat of war illuminated in retrospect the preceding years and revealed that they already belonged to the "new stage of the struggle of the U.S.S.R."[42] where the only thing to do was to take a stand. If he had been arrested a few years earlier[43] or even judged a few months sooner Bukharin would probably have refused to surrender. But in the world situation as of 1938 the liquidation of the opposition can no longer be

[40] *Ibid.*, p. 313.
[41] *Ibid.*, p. 767.
[42] *Ibid.*, p. 779.
[43] He was not arrested earlier and it must be noted that the purge only reached the higher levels of the Party in the years just before the war.

regarded as an accident. Bukharin and his colleagues were
defeated; this means that they were up against a persistent
police force and an implacable dictatorship. But their failure
means something even more essential, namely, that what
broke them was necessitated by that phase of history. "World
history is a world court of judgment,"[44] says Bukharin.

Thus there is a drama in the Moscow Trials but one
which Koestler is far from giving a true presentation. It is
not the Yogi at grips with the Commissar—moral conscience
at grips with political ruthlessness, the oceanic feeling at
grips with action, the heart at grips with logic, the man
without roots at grips with tradition: between these antagonists there is no common ground and consequently no possibility of an encounter. At the most it might happen that in
the same man depending on circumstances the two attitudes
alternate. It is pitiful, but it is nothing more than a psychological case: he can be seen passing from the one attitude
to the other while changing his identity between the two
points. At one moment he is the Yogi and then he forgets
about the necessity we experience of having to externalize
our life in order to realize its truth; at another moment he
reverts to the Commissar and then he is ready to make any
confession. He switches from scientism to the debauches of
the inward life, that is to say, from one idiocy to another. By
contrast, the true nature of tragedy appears once *the same
man* has understood both that he cannot disavow the objective pattern of his actions, that he is what he is for others in
the context of history, and yet that the motive of his actions
constitutes a man's worth as he himself experiences it. In

[44] *Report of Court Proceedings*, p. 778.

this case we no longer have a series of alternations between the inward and the external, subjectivity and objectivity, or judgment and its means but a dialectical relation, that is to say, a contradiction founded in truth, in which the same man tries to realize himself on the two levels.

We are no longer dealing with Rubashov who gives in unconditionally once he falls back into the comradeship of the Party and denies everything including his own past when he hears the cries of Bogrov; we have instead Rubashov who adopts history's viewpoint on himself, and who works for his own condemnation from the side of history while defending his revolutionary honor. Like any man, Bukharin can be understood psychologically. Lenin said of him: he "lends faith to every bit of gossip and he is devilishly *unstable* in politics." And on another occasion: "The war pushed him towards semi-anarchical ideas. At the congress where the Bern resolutions were adopted (in spring 1915) he presented some theses . . . a stock of ineptitudes, a shame, a semi-anarchism." A member of the opposition, rallied to the Stalinist line, again an opposition member, once more realigned with Stalin, Bukharin can and should be understood as an intellectual thrown into politics. If the role of the intellectual and his outlook is to discover in a given assembly of facts several possible meanings to be evaluated methodically, whereas the politician is one who with perhaps the fewest ideas perceives most surely the real significance and pattern in a given situation, Bukharin's instability could then be explained in terms of the intellectual's psychology. Yet, though he oscillates, it is still within the Marxist framework, and this is a constant element in his career which is not therefore to be explained entirely in terms of his professional attitudes.

In the 1938 trials the personal pathos is hidden and a drama transpires that is rooted in the most general structures of human action, the real tragedy of historical contingency. Whatever his goodwill, man undertakes to act without being able to appreciate exactly the objective sense of his action; he constructs his own image of the future which has only a probable basis and in reality solicits that future so that he can be condemned for it because the event in itself is not unequivocal. A dialectic whose course is not entirely foreseeable can transform a man's intentions into their opposite and yet one has to take sides from the very start. In brief, as Napoleon said, and after him Bukharin, before he became silent, "fate is politics,"[45]—destiny here not being a *fatum* already written down unbeknown to us, but the collision in the very heart of history between contingency and the event, between the multiplicity of the eventual and the uniqueness of the necessity in which we find ourselves when acting to treat one of the possibilities as a reality, to regard one of the futures as present. Man can neither suppress his nature as freedom and judgment—what he calls the course of events is never anything but its course as he sees it—nor question the competence of history's tribunal, since in acting he has engaged others and more and more the fate of humanity.

But is it necessary to think along with the rightist opposition that history is moving toward the stabilization of world

45 *Ibid.*, p. 778.

communism, that in this context the U.S.S.R. can only build socialism at home and consequently should retreat and accentuate NEP? Is it necessary, on the contrary, to hold, along with the leftist opposition, that by regarding the stabilization of capitalism as a given, one is strengthening it, and that it is necessary both to build socialism through industrialization and collectivization and adopt the offensive abroad through the agency of a national Communist Party? Is it necessary, finally, to believe with the Stalinist center that in the short interval before the war, history demands that time be gained abroad by an opportunist policy and that the economic buildup of the U.S.S.R. be speeded in every way? History offers us certain factual trends that have to be extrapolated into the future, but it does not give us the knowledge with any deductive certainty of which facts are privileged to outline the present to be ushered in. What is more, at certain moments at least nothing is absolutely fixed by the facts and it is precisely our absence or intervention which history needs in order to take shape. *This does not mean that we can do whatever we please:* there are degrees of probability and these are not nothing. But that means that whatever we do will involve risk. Not that one should hesitate and avoid decisions but that a decision can lead political man to his death and the revolution into failure. Lenin jumped with joy when the Russian Revolution went beyond the time lasted by the Commune. There is a tragedy to the Revolution and the euphoric revolution belongs to Epinal's pictures. This tragedy is aggravated when it comes to knowing not just whether the Revolution will defeat its enemies but between revolutionaries of knowing who has read history best. Finally it is at its height in the case of the member of the opposition who is persuaded that the Revolution is moving in the wrong direction. Thus, there is not just destiny involved—an external force which breaks the will—but genuine tragedy—a man at grips with external forces *with which he is secretly allied*—because the opposition member is unable either to be for nor entirely against the path to power. The split is no longer between man and the world but between man and himself. That is the whole secret of the Moscow confessions.

Bukharin knows that despite everything the infrastructure of a socialist state has to be built up and in the course of its construction he can recognize the basic theme of his former views. Thus he is able to stand aside from it in detachment. And yet he cannot support it fully since he thinks it is on the road to failure. The famous "not with you and not without you," once the formula of a personal sentiment, in History's ambiguous moments becomes the formula for all human action which experiences a metamorphosis into things which it cannot recognize as its own product and yet cannot disavow without contradiction. In politics as in personal relations this forces some to break the pact while others overcome discord out of sheer devotion or pure will power and others again wish neither to break away nor to suffer in silence because in them fidelity and criticism stem from the same principle: they remain faithful to the Party but because they believe in the Revolution as an idea in the mind as well, they criticize the party. This is very well expressed by Bukharin in some remarks made in just such a context:

> . . . everyone of us . . . suffered from a peculiar duality of
> mind, an incomplete faith in his counter-revolutionary cause.
> I will not say that the consciousness of this was absent, but it
> was incomplete. Hence a certain semi-paralysis of the will, a
> retardation of reflexes. . . . And this was due not to the ab-
> sence of consistent thought, but to the objective grandeur of
> socialist construction. . . . A dual psychology arose . . .
>
> Even I was sometimes carried away by the eulogies I wrote
> of socialist construction, although on the morrow I repudiated
> this by practical actions of a criminal character. There arose
> what in Hegel's philosophy is called a most unhappy mind.
> The might of the proletarian state found its expression not
> only in the fact that it smashed the counter-revolutionary
> bands, but also in the fact that it disintegrated its enemies from
> within, that it disorganized the will of its enemies.[46]

According to Hegel, it is true that at the end of history
consciousness should be reconciled with itself. The unhappy
consciousness belonged to an alienated consciousness confronted with a transcendence that it could neither escape
nor assume. Once history had ceased to be a history of rulers
and had become human history, each individual should rediscover himself in the common enterprise and realize himself in it. But even the land of the Revolution has not reached
history's end: the class struggle does not end with a wave of
the magic wand, or with the October Revolution,[47] and the

[46] *Ibid.*, p. 776.
[47] Lenin, *Left-Wing Communism—An Infantile Disorder,* Collected Works,
Vol. 31, Moscow, Progress Publishers, 1966.

unhappy consciousness does not resolve itself by decree. The revolution only gets started with a victorious insurrection, everything lies ahead of it, especially when it occurs in a country where the economic preconditions of socialism are absent. Until the infrastructure has been built up, the unhappy consciousness remains a reality, opposition groups will arise, change sides and take their place in the common endeavor more by an effort of will than a spontaneous movement.

The confessions in the Moscow Trials are only the extreme instance of those letters of submission to the Central Committee which in 1938 were a feature of daily life in the U.S.S.R. They are only mystifying to those who overlook the dialectic between the subjective and objective factors in Marxist politics. "The confession of the accused is a medieval principle of jurisprudence"[48] remarks Bukharin. And yet he confesses his responsibility. The reason is that the Middle Ages are not over, history has not yet ceased to be diabolical, it has not yet driven out its own evil genius and is still capable of mystifying the noble or moral consciousness and turning opposition into treason. To the extent that alienation and transcendence persist, the drama of the opposition member in the Party, is, at least formally, the drama of the heretic in the Church. Not that communism is, as is vaguely said, a religion but because in the one case as in the other the individual acknowledges in advance the jurisdiction of the event, and, having recognized a providential import in the Church, an historical mission in the proletariat and its leadership, having acknowledged that everything that happens is due to

[48] *Report of Court Proceedings*, p. 778.

God or to the logic of history, he can no longer back his own opinion against the judgment of the Party or the Church.

Like the Church, the Party will perhaps rehabilitate those whom it condemned once a new historical phase has altered the significance of their behavior. The sources are there for a personal legitimation: the *Report of Court Proceedings* is available. In it among other things one can see Rykov and Bukharin fighting to keep the proceedings to the statements they made under examination as if there were some contract (explicit or implicit) which held them not to go beyond these limits.[49] One hears Bukharin declare that he is seeing some of his co-defendants for the first time in his life,[50] that others, formerly his friends, are now disowned,[51] and that "the accused in this dock are not a group."[52] If these remarks, translated into every language of the world, were transmitted throughout the world for everyone's attention that is because the People's Commissariat of Justice decided this should be done.

The tragedy of the trials and the sacrifice of Bukharin can be seen from the comparison of two texts. In 1938 Vyshinsky said:

The historic significance of this trial consists before all in the fact that at this trial it has been shown, proved and established with exceptional scrupulousness and exactitude that the Rights, Trotskyites . . . are nothing other than a gang of murderers,

[49] *Ibid.,* pp. 417, 423.
[50] *Ibid.,* p. 769.
[51] *Ibid.,* p. 497.
[52] *Ibid.,* p. 769.

spies, diversionists and wreckers, without any principles or ideals.[53]

Eight years later, after a victorious war, Stalin declared:

It cannot be denied that the Party's politics has run into contradictions. Not only those backward people who always avoid anything new but also a number of people in the fore-front of the Party systematically dragged the Party back-wards and tried with everything in their power to push the Party into the "conventional" capitalist path of development. All the Trotskyite and rightist machinations against its Party and their entire wrecking "activity" directed against our gov-ernment's policies had only one aim: to destroy the Party's program and delay the task of industrialization and collectiviza-tion.[54]

Instead of saying "had only one aim," let us say "could only have one result," or "one meaning," and the discussion is closed.

[53] *Ibid.*, p. 626.

[54] Speech published in *Scanteia,* Central Organ of the Rumanian Communist Party, 13 February, 1946.

III. Trotsky's Rationalism

IF THE MOSCOW TRIALS are understood as a drama of historical responsibility then, to be sure, we are as far from Vyshinsky's interpretation of them as we are from the leftist view. In one of their few agreements both Vyshinsky and Trotsky admit that the Trials raise no problems, the former because the accused are purely and simply guilty and the latter because they are purely and simply innocent. To Vyshinsky, it is a matter of believing the accused's confessions and not believing the reservations that accompanied them. To Trotsky it is a matter of trusting the reservations and nullifying the confessions. They confessed at gun point and because they hoped to save their own lives or the lives of their families, they confessed mainly because they were not true Leninist Bolsheviks, but rightist oppositionists, or "capitulators." For want of a really solid Marxist platform, it was to be expected that they would rally to the Stalinist line every time the country's situation eased and then cross over to the opposition at times of crisis and incipient civil war—

for example, during the period of forced collectivization. They were unstable because their ideas were confused and emotion ruled intellect. But each new reunion became more onerous. In order to regain their place in the Party, each time they had to deny more fully the theses they had maintained just previously. In the end the result was a general mood of skepticism and cynicism which also turned into frivolous criticism and shameless obedience. They were "broken." The case of these innocent capitulators is nothing but a psychological case study. There is no ambivalence in history, there are only irresolute men.

Trotsky knew better than us the character of the men of whom he was speaking. That is the very reason why in regard to the capitulations he abuses the psychological mode of explanation. His acquaintance with the individuals concerned hides from him the historical significance of the events. We have to look beyond psychology, to relate the "capitulations" to the historical phase in which they occur and finally to the very structure of history. The oppositionists who agreed to capitulate and were publicly tried are precisely those most well known, who had played the most important role in the October Revolution (with the exception, of course, of Trotsky himself), and who were probably the most conscientious Marxists. Thus it is hardly reasonable to explain the capitulations solely in terms of weakness of character and political thought, and not rather to believe that they were motivated by their historical situation. In its Stalinist phase the U.S.S.R. was in a position that made it just as difficult for the October generation to support it as to oppose it to the limit. It is an indisputable fact that the

Moscow Trials liquidated the principal representatives of that generation. Zinoviev, Kamenev, Rykov, Bukharin, Trotsky, along with Stalin, comprised Lenin's Politburo. The first two were shot after the trials in 1936, the third after the 1937 trials and the fourth after the trials in 1938. Rykov and Bukharin were still members of the Central Committee in 1936. Piatakov and Radek, also members of the Central Committee, were executed in 1937. They were subpoened by a man who had only lately entered the Party, after the Revolution. Of the six men in the first rank mentioned in Lenin's testament only Stalin remained. All these facts are incontestable and it would surely be strange if Lenin had surrounded himself with supporters all of whom except one were capable of crossing over into the service of capitalist governments.

Any very general opposition would surely have reflected a profound change in the Soviet government's policy. The whole question is to know what this change was and whether Trotsky has understood it correctly. For him it involves the transition from the Revolution to counter-revolution. However, since the Stalinist line proceeded to adopt the leftist platform of industrialization and collectivization, Trotsky is forced to make his criticism more precise. Whether it swings to the left or to the right, the Stalinist line moves through a series of zigzags and not along a truly straight Marxist path. At one moment it beats a retreat (over the issues of foreign policy and world revolution, or internally when it enhances social differences), at another moment it leads a terrorist attack on the remainder of the bourgeoisie (during the period of forced collectivization). In both cases it violates history and for that very rea-

son will run aground, and under the pretext of saving the
Revolution will have liquidated it, as Thermidor and Bonaparte did with the French Revolution. But this is just where
we run into the ambiguity of history which Trotsky refuses
to recognize. For it remains open whether, historically,
Thermidor and Bonaparte destroyed the Revolution or
rather in fact consolidated its results. It is possible that in
the clash of events the radical future of the Revolution is
preserved better through compromise than a radical policy,
just as, in the history of political thought, the Hegelian
compromise had more of a future than Hölderlin's radicalism.

When Trotsky tries as a thoroughgoing Marxist to understand his own failure and the Stalinist consolidation, he is
led to define the present phase as one of a worldwide ebb in
the revolutionary movement. It is inevitable in the dynamics
of the world class struggle that the revolutionary thrust
come to a pause after each surge and that the waves recede
for a time. This is not just an accidental feature, explicable
in terms of the ideas of one or several individuals, or through
the interests of an entrenched bureaucracy; it is an essential
phase in the development of the Revolution. This is the
spirit in which Trotsky's best writings analyze the situation
facing him. *But they either mean nothing, or else they mean
that the theory of the permanent Revolution*—the idea of
a continuous revolutionary effort, a social structure without
inertia and under continuous questioning at the initiative of
the masses, the idea of a transparent and lucid history—*is
much more the expression of Trotsky's rationalism than the
real nature of the revolutionary process.*

For an abstract revolutionary consciousness which turns away from events and hangs on to its goals Napoleon is the liquidator of the Revolution. In reality, along with the violence of military occupation, the Napoleonic armies carried throughout Europe an ideology which later was to make possible a revolutionary resurgence. It would take volumes to establish the historical significance of Thermidor and Bonapartism. It suffices here to show that Trotsky himself describes the Soviet "Thermidor" in such a way that it appears as an ambiguous phase in the History of the Revolution and not the end of it. At the level of universal history it might be regarded as a period of latency during which certain gains are consolidated. Trotsky himself says of Stalin that "Every sentence in his speeches has a practical aim; throughout the discussion never rises to the theoretical level. This weakness constitutes its strength. There are historical tasks which can only be accomplished by forsaking generalizations; there are periods in which generalization and predictions are incompatible with immediate success."[1] In other words, Stalin is a man of our times, which cannot be grasped (as if any age could be entirely) through the "logical construct" of time. The very experience and endowments which qualified the October generation for its historical task now disqualify it for the period we have just entered. From this standpoint, the Moscow Trials might be understood as the drama of a generation which has lost the objective conditions of its own political activity.

Of course, Trotsky would never have accepted this inter-

---

[1] Leon Trotsky, *La Révolution trahie*. Translated from the Russian by Victor Serge, Paris, B. Grasset, 1936–37, Vol. II, *Les Crimes de Staline,* pp. 116–117.

pretation. He would have said that the "objective conditions" in the present period are in part due to Stalinist policies. To take them into account simply involves making things worse. On the other hand one could improve things by initiating a new revolutionary line. As is well known, from 1933 on Trotsky gave up trying to change the Communist Party line from inside the Party and laid the grounds for a Fourth International. But in 1933, Trotsky was deprived of Soviet nationality and exiled. It is questionable whether the effect of being outside the Soviet sphere and forced through exile into an isolated intellectual life did not cause him to underestimate the real constraints and to yield to the intellectual's temptation to schematize history because he does not live at grips with its problems. There is more than a simple hypothesis here. We might compare Trotsky's testimony written while he was still active in Soviet life with that written when he was isolated and cut off from history. If ever there was a moment when the Stalinist line was not entrenched it was in 1926, when Zinoviev and Kamenev broke with Stalin. But at that time Trotsky calculated that the situation inside the U.S.S.R. and abroad made it unlikely that the opposition would come to power.

Early in 1926, when the "new opposition" (Zinoviev-Kamenev) set up talks with my comrades and me about a joint undertaking, Kamenev told me at one of the first chats we had that "it is obvious that the bloc is only viable if you intend to fight to obtain power. We have often wondered whether you were exhausted and had decided to limit yourself to literary criticism instead of fighting." At that time Zinoviev, the great agitator, and Kamenev, the "prudent politician," as Lenin called him, were completely under the illusion that it would be easy for them to regain power. "As soon as they see you on the platform beside Zinoviev," Kamenev said to me, "the Party will cry, 'there it is, Lenin's Central Committee! There's the government!' Everything depends on knowing whether you intend to form a government." Having just emerged from three years of fighting in the opposition (1923–1926) I had no sympathy for these optimistic hopes. Our group ("Trotskyite") had already worked out a clear idea of the second stage of the revolution—Thermidor—the widening gap between the bureaucracy and the people, the nationalist conservative degeneration of the leaders as they became conservative nationalists and the profound repercussions of the defeat of the world proletariat on the destiny of the U.S.S.R. For me the question of power could not be raised in isolation from these basic developments. In the time ahead the role of the opposition would necessarily become a preparatory role. It would be necessary to form new cadres and wait for events. That is what I told Kamenev: "I am not at all 'exhausted,' but it is my view that we have to arm ourselves with patience for a long time to come for a whole historical period. Today's problem is not to fight for power but to prepare the ideological means and the organization for the power struggle in the expectation of a new revolutionary thrust. When that thrust will come, I have no idea."[2]

Thus, on at least one occasion Trotsky yielded to Stalinism as an existing fact and to its leadership as the only possible direction. But in that case can he speak of "political cowardice" when there were others who were joining up

[2] *Les Crimes de Staline,* p. 110.

again? The way he portrays Radek is very convincing and
no one would think of comparing Trotsky's refusal in 1926
to struggle for power with Radek's destruction in 1929 of
what he had adored a few months earlier. The human appeal is not the same in each case, and at the same time there
is something ill-tempered there is also something like envy
in Bukharin's remark at the end of his last appeal: "And one
must be a Trotsky not to lay down one's arms."[3] But history
makes irresolute opponents possible because it is ambiguous
itself; and this ambiguity, though it does not determine but
nevertheless motivates Radek's cowardice, was recognized
by Trotsky the day he gave up overthrowing a leadership
of which he disapproved.

It may be replied that Trotsky never realigned again.
And indeed, when confronted with Zinoviev's dilemma
between being in command or aligning himself, he developed a third possibility—saving the revolutionary heritage,
carrying on agitation everywhere on the classical model
until favorable objective conditions reappeared along with
a new thrust from the masses—in short, adopting the role
of the opposition. But what if circumstances were such that
any opposition would disorganize production? What if
the time allowed the U.S.S.R. for building up its industry
were too short to do so without constraint? What if in the
context of the task undertaken a "humane" politics was
impractical and Terror the only possibility? What if the
dilemma facing Zinoviev and Kamenev—whether to obey
or to rule—expressed the exigencies of the contemporary
situation? What if Trotsky's third possibility was in prin-

---

[3] *Report of Court Proceedings*, p. 778.

ciple excluded by the actual situation? It was in fact and Trotsky was exiled.

At that moment he stopped thinking in terms of "situation." His thought becomes rationalistic and his ethics become Kantian in an almost literal fashion in some remarks in the *Bulletin of the Opposition:* "It is absurd and criminal to play hide-and-seek with the revolution, to deceive the social classes, to play diplomacy with history . . . Zinoviev and Kamenev fell because they failed to observe the only valid principle: to do what must be done no matter what the cost."[4] To be sure, Trotsky is not speaking of duty in the sense of duty toward oneself and others in general, but of duty in the Marxist sense of duty toward the class which has an historical mission. Moreover, the rider "no matter what the cost" should be understood to refer to the immediate future: for Trotsky as for all other Marxists, man realizes himself within history. He simply does not believe that short-run history is all that counts, that no sacrifice is lost since it is incorporated in the proletarian tradition, and when times are unpropitious the revolutionary can always serve by dying for his ideas. "If our generation proves too weak to build socialism on earth, at least we shall have passed on the flag unstained to our children. . . . Under the implacable blows of fate I felt as happy as in the best days of my youth so long as I was contributing to the victory of truth. For the greatest human happiness lies not in the enjoyment of the present but in the preparation of the future." [*Les Crimes de Staline.*] Perhaps here one touches the essence of Trotsky's thought, his lively intuition

[4] *Bulletin de l'Opposition,* October, 1932.

of the future and confrontation with death which is the
existential equivalent of rationalism and, as Hegel saw, the
great temptation for consciousness.

It is well known that Trotsky acted according to his
words and was no mere talker. At the individual level, such
men are sublime. But we have to ask ourselves whether history is made by such men. They have such a tenacious belief
in the rationality of history that when it ceases for a while
to be rational, they throw themselves into the future they
seek rather than have to deal with compromises and incoherence. But to live and die for a future projected by desire
rather than think and act in the present is precisely what
Marxists have always considered utopianism. In the short
run even the price of such intransigence can be high. If
the five-year plans had not been carried out, if the traditional type of military discipline and patriotic propaganda
had not been re-established, can one be sure that the Red
Army would have won? To argue this involves the argument that the exigencies of truth and practicality, the necessities of war and revolution, discipline and humanity not
only converge in the long run, but are identical at every
moment—it means denying the role of contingency in history, whereas Trotsky had always admitted it both as an
historian and a theoretician.[5]

[5] It would be improper to attribute the views of every Trotskyite to Trotsky.
With this reservation, here is an anecdote. During the occupation I remember a
discussion over practicality with a Trotskyite friend, later deported and killed
fighting with the Commandos. He said that it was possible that without Stalin
the U.S.S.R. would have less artillery, but when the Nazis pushed into a country
where a worker's democracy and man's initiative were visible everywhere, they
would have lost in confidence what they gained in territory and everything
would have ended with the formation of Soviets among the soldiers in the

Certain fundamental tenets of Trotskyism show clearly that for Trotsky, as for Marxists in general, politics is not simply a matter of conscience, the simple occasion for subjectivity to express its ideas and values in the world, but the commitment of the abstract moral subject to events that are ambiguous. He understood very well that in certain extreme cases one can only choose for or against, and that is why he maintained until the very end the unconditional defense of the U.S.S.R. in wartime.

On this point, and the recent collection published in New York (L. Trotsky, *In Defense of the Soviet Union,* New York, Pioneer Publishers, 1937) is testimony, I have always and without wavering fought the least hesitation. On more than one occasion I have had to break with friends over this issue. In *The Revolution Betrayed,* I show that the war endangered not just the bureaucracy but also the new social foundations of the U.S.S.R. which represent an immense advance in human history. From this there follows, for every revolutionary, the absolute duty of defending the U.S.S.R. against imperialism, despite the Soviet bureaucracy [*Les Crimes de Staline*].

This defense of the U.S.S.R. differs from a realignment inasmuch as Trotsky intended to continue to agitate at the height of the war in favor of his own views, just as Clemenceau set up an opposition until the conduct of the war was

---

German army. This is an example of what is called abstract history. Trotsky's "no matter what the cost," is preferable at least for showing more awareness. But if there has to be a choice between a U.S.S.R. which "connives with history," maintains its existence and stops the Germans and a U.S.S.R. which sticks to the proletarian line and is crushed in war, leaving future generations with an example of heroism and fifty years of more Nazism, is it political cowardice to prefer the former case?

handed over to him. But is this restriction compatible with the thesis of the defense of the U.S.S.R.? Perhaps in an advanced, democratic country the conduct of a war is quite compatible with the existence of an opposition. But in a country just emerging from forced collectivization and industrialization, the existence of an organized opposition which aims at the overthrow of the revolutionary leadership poses quite different problems. To take for granted that such a thing is possible involves a claim that it is always possible to discriminate finely, that one is never forced to answer yes or no, to be thoroughly for or against, that there always remains a certain margin of freedom. The principle of the defense of the U.S.S.R. is grounded in the opposite principle. But how does one delimit an emergency? The danger starts before war is declared. Thus there is a whole series of transitions between the principle of the defense of the U.S.S.R. and the platform of the "capitulators." In refusing to follow the extreme left and acknowledging that the revolutionary will and the subjective factor cannot disassociate themselves from the economic structure established by the October Revolution, Trotsky admits in this case that radicalism might become counterrevolutionary and rejoins Bukharin. The difference is one of degree and not in kind. True, beyond a certain point, quantity changes into quality and to form a bloc is not the same thing as to capitulate. But in its own way Bukharin's last plea reveals as much pride as Trotsky writing in exile. The left has its extreme left which accuses it as well of "political cowardice."[6]

[6] More recently, wherever the elements of the Fourth International did not present candidates they instructed the voters to vote Communist because to

To the extent that Trotsky became removed from action and power and saw the U.S.S.R. no longer from the standpoint of one in the government but from the side of a hunted opposition and those who are ruled, he was inclined to idealize the past—the past in which he had a hand—and to blacken the present stage of history in which he was not active. It is tempting to read to the opposition the striking passages Trotsky wrote in 1920 in defense of dictatorship. They would counter that in 1920 it was the dictatorship of the proletariat of which the Party was only the conscious element and the leaders elected representatives and that consequently, at least within the Party, there was room for revolutionary brotherhood. Though the Party was acting not with the express mandate of present humanity but at least as the delegate of the proletariat as the core of future humanity, the dictatorship was established to employ violence against the class enemy, the obstacle to the future. It had no need to use violence against the proletariat and its political representatives.

This conception of the dictatorship of the proletariat calls for a complete analysis. One would have to ask whether the dictatorship *of the proletariat* ever existed anywhere but in the minds of the leaders and the most active militants. Next to the militants, there were the masses who had no awareness. *In its own eyes,* the dictatorship might well be a dictatorship of the proletariat—but the apolitical worker

---

them the Communist candidates were still proletarian candidates. In principle, the Trotskyites ran the risk of bringing to power a political machine which according to Trotsky sabotages the Revolution, but, under present conditions, has still to be chosen. There is no *essential* difference between this tactic and Bukharin's platform.

or the backward peasant could recognize themselves in it only during brief moments of the Revolution. The party is the conscience of the proletariat, but since everyone admits that the proletariat is not awake as a whole, a segment of the proletariat therefore thinks and wills by proxy. There is no doubt that at several decisive moments in the Russian Revolution the Party resolutions went beyond the existing will of the masses (just as at other times the Party restrained the masses). To that extent the Party substituted itself for the masses and its role was more to explicate and legitimate decisions already arrived at rather than to seek the proletariat's opinion.

Lenin thought that the Party should not be behind the proletariat, nor beside it, but rather ahead of it, though only one step ahead. This famous phrase[7] shows how far he was from any theory of revolution from the top. But it also shows that the revolutionary leadership always involved control, and if it had to be followed by the masses, it was necessary for it to precede them. The Party leads the existing proletariat in the name of an idea of the proletariat which it draws from its philosophy of history and which does not coincide at every moment with the will and sentiment of the proletariat at present. Lenin and his comrades did what the masses wanted in the depths of their will and to the extent of their self-awareness; but to act according to someone's deepest convictions, such as one has defined them, is precisely to force him, as when a father forbids his son a foolish marriage "for his own good." The proletariat

[7] "One Step Forward, Two Steps Back," V. I. Lenin, *Selected Works*, Vol. II, London, Lawrence and Wishart Ltd., 1936.

does not want to exercise its dictatorship itself and so it delegates its powers. Either one wants to make a revolution, in which case one has to handle what it involves, or else one seeks at every moment to treat every man as an end in himself, and then one does nothing at all.

Thus we are not reproaching Trotsky with having used violence in his time, but of forgetting it, and of using the arguments of formal humanism against the dictatorship which now rules him when they once seemed false to him applied to the dictatorship he exercised. Is it because the early dictatorship employed violence against the class enemy, whereas the present one uses it against former Bolsheviks? Or maybe in the present situation the opposition plays the role of the class enemy. Formally, dictatorship is dictatorship. Undoubtedly, the content has varied—we shall return to that—but there is an imperceptible and more or less conscious transition from the dictatorship of 1920 to that of 1935. That is what we have to start by seeing.

In 1920 Trotsky wrote: "The foundations of the militarization of labor are those forms of State compulsion without which the replacement of capitalist economy by the Socialist will forever remain an empty sound."[8] He defended the principle of an authoritarian management of the factories over that of the workers' control, the idea of a "labor front," the obligation of workers to work in positions assigned to them. Those who disobeyed would be deprived of their rations.

[8] L. Trotsky, *Terrorism and Communism,* A Reply to Karl Kautsky. Foreword and Translation by Max Shachtman, Ann Arbor, The University of Michigan Press, 1961, p. 141.

In point of fact, under Socialism there will not exist the apparatus of compulsion itself, namely the State: for it will have melted away entirely into a producing and consuming commune. Nonetheless, the road to Socialism lies through a period of the highest possible intensification of the principle of the State . . . just as a lamp, before going out, shoots up in a brilliant flame, so the State, before disappearing, assumes the form of the dictatorship of the proletariat, i.e., the most ruthless form of State, which embraces the life of the citizens authoritatively in every direction.[9]

And what about political freedom? If it were observed scrupulously it would turn into its opposite. A Constituent Assembly with an opportunist majority was elected in 1917.

If we take the viewpoint of isolated historical possibilities, one might say that it would have been more painless if the Constituent Assembly had worked for a year or two, had finally discredited the Socialist Revolutionaries and the Mensheviks by their connection with the Cadets, and had thereby led to the formal majority of the Bolsheviks, showing the masses that in reality only two forces existed; the revolutionary proletariat led by the Communists, and the counter-revolutionary democracy, headed by the generals and the admirals. But the point is that the pulse of the internal relations of the revolution was beating not at all in time with the pulse of the development of its external relations. If our party had thrown all responsibility on to the objective formula of "the course of events" the development of military operations might have forestalled us. German imperialism might have seized Petrograd, the evacuation of which the Kerensky Government had already begun. The fall of Petrograd would at that time have

[9] *Ibid.*, pp. 169–170.

meant a death-blow to the proletariat, for all the best forces of the revolution were concentrated there, in the Baltic Fleet and in the Red capital.

Our party may be accused, therefore, not of going against the course of historical development, but of having taken at a stride several political steps. It stepped over the heads of the Mensheviks and the Socialist-Revolutionaries, in order not to allow German imperialism to step across the head of the Russian proletariat and conclude peace with the entente on the back of the revolution before it was able to spread its wings over the world.[10]

But then one can say that Stalin overruled the opposition in order to prevent German militarism from thwarting the only country in which socialist forms of production had been established.

And what about freedom of the press? Kautsky had defended it in the name of the indisputable idea that there is no absolute truth that any individual or group can boast of possessing, and that liars and fanatics of (what they take to be) the truth are to be found in both camps. To which Trotsky replies in the following lively remarks:

> In this way, in Kautsky's eyes, the revolution, in its most acute phase, when it is a question of the life and death of classes, continues as hitherto to be a literary discussion with the object of establishing . . . the truth. What profundity! . . . Our "truth," of course, is not absolute. But as in its name we are, at the present moment, shedding our blood, we have neither cause nor possibility to carry on a literary discussion as to the relativity of truth with those who "criticize" us with

[10] *Ibid.*, p. 43

the help of all forms of arms. Similarly, our problem is not to punish liars and to encourage just men amongst journalists of all shades of opinion, but to throttle the class lie of the bourgeoisie and to achieve the class truth of the proletariat, irrespective of the fact that in both camps there are fanatics and liars.[11]

The ideas for which one lives and dies are by this very fact absolutes and one cannot at the same time treat them as relative truths which might be calmly compared with others and "literally criticized." But if Trotsky, in the name of his own absolute, rejects the Menshevik's absolute as merely relative, then he should hardly be surprised that in turn they should do the same to Trotsky from their standpoint. Trotsky brings to light the element of subjectivity and Terror contained in every revolution, even a Marxist one. But in that case any critique of Stalinism which questions Terror formally can be applied to the Revolution in general.

When he was in power Trotsky had a vivid awareness that although history as a whole can be seen from the perspective of the history of class struggles, to reach its revolutionary goal it must at every moment be thought through and willed by individuals; and although there are privileged moments in history, lost occasions can alter the course of events for a long time and so must be seized when they offer themselves, even if there is not always time to persuade the masses first; and, finally, that history has to be made through violence and does not make itself. Somewhere he relates that one day while he and Lenin were working together, he asked Lenin: "If they shoot us, what will become of the Revolution?" Lenin thought a moment, smiled and

11 *Ibid.*, p. 60.

said simply: "Perhaps after all they will not shoot us." Even if a revolution is "in the path of history," it needs individual initiative. Kautsky claimed that Russia was a backward country to which the proletarian revolution came too soon, and that it would have been better to let her mature than to force history and to set the Russian proletariat on a road where it could only succeed through violence. One should know something about a locomotive before setting it in motion. To this Trotsky replied that if one waits to get to know a horse before mounting, one never mounts. "For the fundamental Bolshevik prejudice is precisely this: that one learns to ride on horseback only when sitting on the horse."[12]

Thus history is not comparable to a machine, but to a living being. There is a science of the revolution, but there is also a revolutionary *praxis* which that science clarifies but does not replace. There is a spontaneous movement of objective history, but there is also human intervention which makes it leap stages and which cannot be foretold from theoretical schemas. All this, Trotsky knew very well, like all the others who in 1917 *made* a revolution whose possibility they perceived from day to day, although the general forecasts favored an intermediary phase of the liberal-democratic type. But then he can only criticize the violence of collectivization by applying to Stalin Kautsky's arguments against Bolshevism. Earlier he had said that there was not an atom of Marxism in Kautsky's views, for instead of the class struggle he believed in "a belated piece of rationalism in the spirit of the eighteenth century,"[13]

12 *Ibid.*, p. 101.
13 *Ibid.*, p. 27.

that is to say, in a continuous progress without violence
toward the classless society; "all history resolves itself into
an endless sheet of printed paper, and the centre of this
'humane' process proves to be the well-worn writing table
of Kautsky."[14] At that time Trotsky understood very well
that history is not made in advance, that it depends on the
will and audacity of men upon occasion, and that it contains
an element of contingency and risk.

The political worshippers of routine, incapable of surveying
the historical process in its complexity, in its internal clashes
and contradictions, imagined to themselves that history was
preparing the way for the Socialist order simultaneously and
systematically on all sides, so that concentration of production
and the development of a Communist morality in the producer
and the consumer mature simultaneously with the electric
plough and a parliamentary majority.[15]

Certainly Trotsky never deluded himself about parliamentary majorities. But he believed that socialism took root
everywhere at once; he based all his politics on the coordi-
nation of revolutionary movements and refused to admit
the fact of the revolution in one country—or in any case
to draw the consequences. He regarded the worldwide revolutionary stagnation as an accident which hardly changed
the Party line. In short, in the latter part of his life he acted
as though there were no contingencies and as though the
ambiguity of events, cunning, and violence had been elimi-
nated from history. In 1920 he wrote:

14 *Ibid.,* p. 27.
15 *Ibid.,* p. 16.

The man who repudiates terrorism in principle—i.e., repudiates measures of suppression and intimidation towards determined and armed counter-revolution, must reject all idea of the political supremacy of the working class and its revolutionary dictatorship. The man who repudiates the dictatorship of the proletariat repudiates the Socialist revolution, and digs the grave of Socialism.[16]

But if propaganda is a weapon and leftism sometimes counterrevolutionary, then it is difficult to delimit permissible Terror. There are all kinds of gradations between a Trotskyite dictatorship and a Stalinist dictatorship, and between Lenin's line and Stalin's line there is no difference that is an *absolute* difference. Nothing allows us to say precisely: here Marxist politics end and there counterrevolution begins.

The Terror of History culminates in Revolution and History is Terror because there is contingency. Everyone looks through the facts for his motives and then erects a schematization of the future which cannot be strictly proved. Trotsky conceives the direction of the Revolution as a junction of the class struggle and the major trends of universal history. Stalin constructed his policies as a function of the circumstances peculiar to our times: socialism in one country, fascism, and the stabilization of Western capitalism. In saying that Stalinist developments began with the failure of the German revolution in 1923,[17] Trotsky at least recognizes

---

[16] *Ibid.*, p. 23.

[17] "If, at the end of 1923, the revolution had been victorious in Germany—which was quite possible—the dictatorship of the proletariat in Russia would have been refined and consolidated without internal upheavals." *La Défense de l'U.R.S.S. et l'Opposition*, Paris, Librairie du Travail, 1930, pp. 28–29.

that they take account of historical circumstances. Under these conditions each side can accuse the other of "digging the grave of the revolution." Trotsky speaks of the Stalinist counterrevolution. But, in the light of the way the bourgeoisie turns the Trotskyite criticism, Bukharin in his final plea remarked that "in the parallelogram of forces which went to make up the counter-revolutionary tactics, Trotsky was the principal motive force."

There might be an absolute truth which would divide the antagonists if ever there was an end to history and the world. Once everything was over, then and only then could reality and possibility become identical because there would be nothing beyond the past. In that case there could be no sense in saying that had men behaved differently, history would have been different; from the standpoint of the end of history, of a finished world, these other possibilities become imaginary and every conceivable thing is reduced to something which has existed. But the point is that we are not spectators of a closed history; we are actors in an open history, our *praxis* introduces the element of construction rather than knowledge as an ingredient of the world, making the world not simply an object of contemplation but something to be transformed. What we cannot imagine is a consciousness without a future and a history with an end. Thus, as long as there are men, the future will be open and there will only be a probabilistic calculation and no absolute knowledge. Consequently "the dictatorship of the truth" will always be the dictatorship of a group, and to those who do not share it, it will appear purely arbitrary. A revolution, even when founded on a philosophy of history, is a forced revolution and it is violence; correlatively, opposition in the name of humanism can be counterrevolutionary. As an exiled leader, Trotsky might very well miss this point. Those who stayed and fought on could see it. "We would be running a criminal risk in setting the half-starved, backward and unenlightened workers against their own organized avant-garde, which, however weak and exhausted, is all they have. . . . In trying to renew the revolution we would risk unleashing the forces hostile to the peasant masses."[18] The irony of fate drives us to do the opposite of what we think we will do; it forces us to doubt our senses, to impugn our proneness to mystification, and brings to light not just the terror which each man holds for every other man but, above all, that basic Terror in each of us which comes from the awareness of his historical responsibility.

To align or to revolt—Rubashov's problem is a real one, since there are reasons why both Bukharin and Trotsky should dispute the Party line, reasons for Bukharin to rejoin the Party, and reasons for Stalin to "overstep" the opposition if he wanted to save the future of the Revolution, without anyone being able in the name of a science of history to accord any of these positions the privilege of absolute truths. These political divergences within the Marxist philosophy are hardly surprising. Marxist action aims simultaneously at following the spontaneous movement of history and transforming it. Nothing in the facts points in an *obvious* way to the time when one should bow before them or, on the contrary, do violence to them. Our standpoint, and the

18 Victor Serge, *S'il est minuit dans le Siècle,* Paris, B. Grasset, 1939, p. 231.

"only possible solution" seen from it, expresses a decision that has already been made, just as our decisions translate the style of the historical landscape around us. Finally, that *operative knowledge,* whose general formula is given by Marxism, must continuously examine itself and painfully struggle along a path that turns neither toward opportunism nor utopianism.

History is Terror because we have to move into it not by any straight line that is always easy to trace, but by taking our bearings at every moment in a general situation which is changing, like a traveler who moves into a changing countryside continuously altered by his own advance, where what looked like an obstacle becomes an opening and where the shortest path turns out the longest. A social reality which is never detached from us, or self-determined like an object, and which belongs to our *praxis* for the whole extent of the present and the future, does not offer one unique possibility at each moment, as if God had already fixed the future from behind the world scene. Even the success of a policy does not prove that it was the only successful possibility. Perhaps some other line would have appeared equally possible had someone chosen it and followed it through. Thus it appears that history does not so much pose problems as enigmas.

But this is just a start and only a half truth. It is possible to see ambiguity and contingency at the heart of history and then to "understand" the protagonists in the drama, to relate every view of history to decisions that are optional in the strict sense, and finally to conclude that it is not a matter of being right—since the present and the future are not the object of a science but of *construction* or *action*. But such irrationalism is indefensible for the decisive reason that *no one lives it, not even he who professes it.* The philosopher who abstractly takes up one opinion after another can find nothing in them to separate them radically and concludes that history is terror. He then adopts a spectator standpoint which employs terror merely as a literary device. He thus fails to notice that this outlook is related to the precise circumstances of being a mind in isolation and to the quite particular prejudice of trotting from one perspective to another and never settling on any one. In this manner such an historian himself acquires an historical outlook and understands everything except that others as well as himself can have an historical *perspective*.

Stalin, Trotsky, and even Bukharin each had a perspective within the ambiguity of history and each staked his life upon it. The future is only probable but it is not any empty zone in which we can construct gratuitous projects; it is sketched before us like the beginning of the day's end, and its outline is ourselves. The objects of perception are likewise only probable since we are far from having a complete analysis of them; that does not mean that in their very nature and existence they appear to be absolutely under our control. For us the probability that characterizes objects is what is real and one can only devalue it with reference to the chimera of an apodictic certainty which has no grounds in any human experience. What should be said is not that "everything is relative," but that "everything is absolute"; the simple fact that man perceives an historical situation as meaningful in a way he believes true introduces a phenomenon of truth of which skepticism has no account and which challenges its conclusions. The contingency of history is only a shadow at the edge of a view of the future from which we can no more refrain than we can from breathing. The way we perceive depends upon our wishes and our values, but the reverse is also true; we love or hate not just in terms of previous values but from experience, from what we see, from our historical experience; and even if every historical choice is subjective, every subjectivity nevertheless reaches through its phantasms to things themselves and aims at the truth. Any description of history as the confrontation of choices that cannot be justified omits the fact that every conscience experiences itself engaged with others in a common history, argues in order to convince them, weighs and compares its own chances and those of others, and in seeing itself bound to others through external circumstances establishes the grounds of a presumptive rationality upon which their argument can take place and acquire a meaning. The dialectic of the subjective and the objective is not a simple contradiction which leaves the terms it plays on disjointed; it is rather a testimony to our rootedness in the truth.

In more concrete terms, the common assumption of all revolutionaries is that the contingency of the future and the role of human decisions in history makes political divergences irreducible and cunning, deceit and violence inevitable. In this respect, Trotsky, Bukharin, and Stalin are all opposed to the liberal ethics because it presupposes a given humanity, whereas they aim at making humanity. Once the anarchist (and in any case impractical) principle of unconditional respect for others has been abandoned, it is difficult to mark the limits of legitimate violence; in particular there exists a whole series of transitions from Leninism to Stalinism. This means that when confronted with the problem of violence we find no *absolute* difference between the various Marxist policies. That does not mean that we identify them all, or that we justify them all or even that we can justify none of them.

So far we have limited the terms of our discussion: we now know that there can be no question of simply facing the revolutionary with the principle of absolute nonviolence which ultimately rests on the idea of a world that is *well and truly made.* In resuming the debate between the right, left, and center Communists, we have placed ourselves in the unfinished world of the revolutionary, which as we have seen is a world of Terror for everyone and in this respect allows of no difference in principle between policies. But, having done this, and adopting the relativist standpoint at present (which is the only one from which there can be human discussion), we have still to ask whether the violence which is common to Marxist policies has in every case the same meaning and whether that meaning is clear enough for us to be able to adopt one of these policies. For it is certain that neither Bukharin nor Trotsky nor Stalin regarded Terror as intrinsically valuable. Each one imagined he was using it to realize a genuinely human history which had not yet started but which provides the justification for revolutionary violence. In other words, as Marxists, all three confess that there is a meaning to such violence—that it is possible to understand it, to read into it a rational development and to draw from it a humane future.

Marxism does not offer us a utopia, a future known ahead of time, nor any philosophy of history. However, it deciphers events, discovers in them a common meaning and thereby grasps a leading thread which, without dispensing us from fresh analysis at every stage, allows us to orient ourselves toward events. Marxism is as foreign to a dogmatic philosophy of history which seeks to impose by fire and sword a visionary future of mankind as it is to a terrorism lacking all perspective. It seeks, rather, to offer men a *perception of history* which would continuously clarify the lines of force and vectors of the present. Consequently, if Marxism is a theory of violence and a justification of Terror, it brings reason out of unreason, and the violence which it legitimates should bear a sign which distinguishes it from regressive forms of violence. Whether one is a Marxist or not, one cannot consistently live with or proclaim pure violence apart from any perspective on the future. In the end it is excluded by the theoretical perspectives of Marxism just as in the present it is outlawed by the pledge of beautiful souls.

Therefore we have to situate the crises in the Russian Communist Party in the framework that is common to the Soviet government and its antagonists and to inquire whether from this perspective violence is not the infantile disorder of a new history or merely an episode in an unchanging history.

Part Two: The Humanist Perspective

IV. From the Proletarian to the Commissar

THE FOUNDATIONS of Marxist politics are to be found *simultaneously* in the inductive analysis of the economic process and in a certain intuition of man and the relations between men. "To be radical," says Marx in a well-known passage, "is to grasp things by the root. But for man the root is man himself."[1] Marx's innovation does not lie in the reduction of philosophical and human problems to problems of economics but in drawing from economics the real equivalents of these questions. It has been remarked without paradox that *Capital* is a concrete *Phenomenology of Mind,* that is to say, that it is inseparably concerned with the working of the economy and the realization of man. The point of connection between these two problem areas lies in the Hegelian idea that every system of production and property implies a system of relations between men such that their social relations become imprinted upon their relations to nature, and these in turn imprint upon *their* social relations. There can be no definitive understanding of the whole im-

[1] *Contribution to the Critique of Hegel's Philosophy of Right.*

port of Marxist politics without going back to Hegel's description of the fundamental relations between men.

"Each self-consciousness aims at the destruction and death of the other," says Hegel.[2] Inasmuch as self-consciousness gives meaning and value to every object that we can grasp, it is by nature in a state of vertigo and it is a permanent temptation for it to assert itself as the expense of other consciousnesses who dispute its privilege. But consciousness can do nothing without its body and can only act upon others by acting on their bodies. It can only reduce them to slavery by making nature an appendix of its body, by appropriating nature to itself and establishing in nature its instruments of power. Thus history is essentially a struggle—the struggle of the master and the slave, the struggle between classes—and this is a necessity of the human condition; because of the fundamental paradox that man is an indivisible consciousness no one is able to affirm himself except by reducing the others to objects.

What accounts for there being a human history is that man is a being who externalizes himself, who needs others and nature to fulfill himself, who individualizes himself by appropriating certain goods and thereby enters into conflict with other men. Man's self-oppression may appear unmasked, as in despotism, where the absolute subjectivity of one individual transforms all others into objects; it may be disguised in the dictatorship of objective truth, as in those regimes which imprison, burn, and hang their citizens for their salvation (though the disguise is useless since an imposed truth is only the truth of a few, i.e., the instrument

2 *The Phenomenology of Mind,* p. 232 (Translator).

of their power); finally, violence as in the liberal state, may be put outside the law and, in effect, suppressed in the commerce of ideas though maintained in daily life in the form of colonization, unemployment, and wages. In every case we are only dealing with different modalities of the same fundamental situation. What Marxism undertakes is a radical solution to the problem of human coexistence beyond the oppression of absolute subjectivity and absolute objectivity, and beyond the pseudo-solution of liberalism.

To the extent that it gives a pessimistic picture of our starting point—conflict and struggle to the death—Marxism will always contain an element of violence and Terror. If it is true that history is a struggle, if rationalism is itself a class ideology, there is no possibility of reconciling men very soon through an appeal to what Kant called a "good will," or a universal ethic free from conflict. "We must be able to stand up to all this, agree to make any sacrifice, and even— if need be—to resort to various stratagems, artifices and illegal methods, to evasions and subterfuges, as long as we get into the trade unions, remain in them and carry on communist work within them at all costs."[3] And Trotsky has the following comment: "The life and death struggle is unthinkable without military craftiness, in other words, without lying and deceit."[4]

To tell the truth and to act out of conscience are nothing but alibis of a false morality; true morality is not concerned with what we think or what we want but obliges us to take

[3] V. I. Lenin, *Left-Wing Communism—An Infantile Disorder, loc. cit.*, Vol. 31, p. 55.

[4] "Their Morals and Ours," *The Basic Writings of Trotsky*. Edited and Introduced by Irving Howe, New York, Random House, 1963, p. 394.

an historical view of ourselves. Thus the Communist disturbs conscience: in himself and in others. Consciousness is not a good judge of what we are *doing* since we are involved in the struggle of history and in this we achieve more, less, or something else than we thought we were doing. As a rule, the Communist does not allow himself to trust others at their word or to treat them as free and rational subjects. How could he, since they are exposed as he himself is to mystification? He wants to uncover what they are behind what they think and say deliberately, the role they are playing, perhaps unwittingly, in the clash of forces and the class struggle. He has to learn to recognize the play of opposing forces, and those writers, even the reactionary ones, who have described it are more precious for communism than those, however progressive, who have masked it with liberal illusions. Machiavelli is worth more than Kant. Engels said that Machiavelli was "the first writer of modern times worth mention." Marx said of the *History of Florence* that it was a "master-piece." He considered Machiavelli, with Spinoza, Rousseau, and Hegel, in the company of those who had discovered the working laws of the State.[5] As social life in general affects each individual beyond his deliberate thoughts and decisions down to the very manner of his being in the world, the Revolution in the Marxist sense is not exhausted by the legislative actions it takes; it takes a long time for it to extend from its economic and legal infrastructures into the lived relations of men—a long time therefore before it can really be indisputable and guaranteed against harmful reversals to the old world. During this

5 *Kölnische Zeitung*, No. 179.

transitional period the application of the philosophical rule that "man is the supreme being for man" (Marx) would be a reversion to utopia and would in reality achieve the opposite of what we intended.

If it is true that the state as we know it is the instrument of a class, we may assume that it "will wither away" with the disappearance of classes. But Lenin carefully points out that "it has never entered the head of any socialist to 'promise' that the higher phase of the development of Communism will arrive."[6] This means that Marxism, rather than an affirmation of a future that is necessary, is much more a judgment of the present as contradictory and intolerable. It operates in the tangle of the present and with the means of action offered by the present. The proletariat cannot destroy the machinery of bourgeois oppression without first seizing it and turning it against the bourgeoisie. The result is that Communist action disavows at the outset the formal rules of the bourgeoisie. "So long as the proletariat still uses the state," says Engels, "it does not use it in the interests of freedom but in order to hold down its adversaries, and as soon as it becomes possible to speak of freedom the state as such does not exist."[7] And Lenin remarks: "It is clear that there is no freedom and no democracy where there is suppression and where there is violence."[8] He goes on to say that:

It is not a matter of observing the rules of liberalism in relation to the bourgeoisie, still less with respect to the proletariat as a

---

[6] V. I. Lenin, "The State and Revolution," *Collected Works,* Vol. 25, p. 469.

[7] Engels to Bebel, 18–28 March, 1875, in Karl Marx and Friedrich Engels, *Correspondence, 1846–1895.* Translated by Dona Torr, London, Lawrence and Wishart Ltd., 1936.

[8] V. I. Lenin, "The State and Revolution," *loc. cit.,* p. 462.

whole. Classes still remain, and will remain everywhere *for years after* the proletariat's conquest of power. . . . The abolition of classes means not merely ousting the landowners and the capitalists—that is something we accomplished with comparative ease; it also means *abolishing the small commodity producers* and they *cannot be ousted,* or crushed; we *must learn to live with them.* They can (and must) be transformed and reeducated only by means of very prolonged, slow, and cautious organizational work. They surround the proletariat on every side with a petty bourgeois atmosphere, which permeates and corrupts the proletariat, and constantly causes among the proletariat relapses into petty-bourgeois spinelessness, disunity, individualism, and alternating moods of exaltation and dejection. The strictest centralization and discipline are required within the political party of the proletariat in order to counteract this. . . . The dictatorship of the proletariat means a persistent struggle—bloody and bloodless, violent and peaceful, military and economic, educational and administrative—against the forces and traditions of the old society. The force of habit on millions and tens of millions is a most formidable force. Without a party of iron that has been tempered in the struggle, a party enjoying the confidence of *all honest people* in the class in question, a party capable of watching and influencing the mood of the masses, such a struggle cannot be waged successfully.[9]

It is understandable that in the organization of "democratic centralism" the proportions of democracy and centralism might vary according to circumstances and that at certain moments it can approach pure centralism. The Party and its

---

[9] V. I. Lenin, *Left-Wing Communism—An Infantile Disorder, loc. cit.,* pp. 44–45.

leaders lead the masses toward their real liberty, which is still to come, by sacrificing formal liberty, if necessary, which is everyday liberty. But from this point on, for the entire period of revolutionary transformation (and we do not know if it will ever end in a "higher phase" where the State has withered away), are we not very close to the Hegelian concept of the State, that is, a system which in the last analysis reserves to a few the role of *subjects of history,* the rest remaining the *objects* of this transcendental will?

To such questions the immediate response of Marxism is: it is either that or nothing. Either one wants to do something, but it is on condition of using violence—or else one respects formal liberty and renounces violence, but one can only do this by renouncing socialism and the classless society, in other words by consolidating the rule of "Quaker hypocrisy." The Revolution takes on and directs a violence which bourgeois society tolerates in unemployment and in war and disguises with the name of misfortune. But successful revolutions taken altogether have not spilled as much blood as the empires. All we know is different kinds of violence and we ought to prefer revolutionary violence because it has a future of humanism.

All the same, what does the future of the Revolution matter if its present remains under the law of violence? Even if in the end it produces a society without violence, in respect of those whom it crushes today, each of whom is a world to himself, it is absolutely evil. Even if those who will inhabit the future can one day talk of success, those who live at present and are unable to make the transition have only a failure to record. Revolutionary violence does not make itself distinct *for us* from other kinds of violence and social life only involves failures.

The argument and its conclusion would be valid if history was the simple encounter and discreet succession of absolutely autonomous individuals, without roots, without posterity, without any interaction. In this case, the good of some could not redeem the evil to others and where each conscience is a totality unto itself, the violence done to a single conscience would suffice, as Péguy thought, to damn the society that caused it. There would be no sense in preferring a regime which employed violence for humanist aims since from the viewpoint of the conscience which suffers it, violence is absolutely unacceptable, being the negation of conscience; and in such a philosophy there can be no other standpoint than that of self-consciousness, the world and history being only the sum of such viewpoints. But these are precisely the axioms that Marxism, following Hegel, questions by introducing the perspective of one consciousness upon another. What we find in the private life of a couple, or in a society of friends, or, with all the more reason, in history, is not a series of juxtaposed "self-consciousnesses."

I never encounter face to face another person's consciousness any more than he meets mine. I am not for him and nor is he for me a pure existence for itself. We are both for one another situated beings, characterized by a certain type of relation to men and the world, by a certain activity, a certain way of treating other people and nature. Of course, a pure consciousness would be in such a state of *original innocence* that any harm done to him would be irreparable. But to start with a pure consciousness is beyond my grasp; even if I tortured his body I could not do him any violence. In such a case the problem of violence does not arise. It only arises with respect to a consciousness originally committed in the world, that is to say, with violence, and thus can only be solved beyond utopia. We only know of situated consciousnesses which blend themselves with the situation they take and are unable to complain at being identified with it or at the neglect of the incorruptible innocence of conscience. When one says that there is a history one means precisely that each person committing an act does so not only in his own name, engages not only himself, but also others whom he makes use of, so that as soon as we begin to live, we lose the alibi of good intentions; we are what we do to others, we yield the right to be respected as noble souls. To respect one who does not respect others is ultimately to despise them; to abstain from violence toward the violent is to become their accomplice.

We do not have a choice between purity and violence but between different kinds of violence. Inasmuch as we are incarnate beings, violence is our lot. There is no persuasion even without seduction, or in the last analysis, contempt. Violence is the common origin of all regimes. Life, discussion, and political choice occur only against a background of violence. What matters and what we have to discuss is not violence but its sense or its future. It is a law of human action that the present encroaches upon the future, the self upon other people. This intrusion is not only a fact of political life it also happens in private life. Just as in love, in affection, or in friendship we do not encounter face to face "consciousnesses" whose absolute individuality we could respect at every moment, but beings qualified as "my son," "my wife," "my friend" whom we carry along with us into common projects where they receive (like ourselves) a definite role, with specific rights and duties, so in collective history the spiritual atoms train after them their historical role and are tied to one another by the threads of their actions; what is more, they are blended with the totality of actions, whether or not deliberate, which they exert upon others and the world so that there exists not a plurality of subjects, but an intersubjectivity, and that is why there exists a common measure of the evil inflicted upon certain people and of the good gotten out of it by others.

He who condemns all violence puts himself outside the domain to which justice and injustice belong. He puts a curse upon the world and humanity—a hypocritical curse, since he who utters it has already accepted the rules of the game from the moment that he has begun to live. Between men considered as pure consciousnesses there would indeed be no reason to choose. But between men considered as the incumbents of situations which together compose a single *common situation* it is inevitable that one has to choose—it is allowable to sacrifice those who according to the logic of their situation are a threat and to promote those who offer a promise of humanity. This is what Marxism does when it creates its politics on the basis of an analysis of the situation of the proletariat.

Political problems come from the fact that we are all subjects and yet we look upon other people and treat them as objects. Coexistence among men seems therefore doomed to failure. For either some men exercise their absolute right as subjects in which case the others submit to their will and are not recognized as subjects. Or else the whole social body is devoted to some providential destiny, some philosophical mission, but then this case reverts to the first; objective politics becomes subjective politics since it is really necessary that only a few be the incumbents of this destiny or mission. Or finally it is agreed that all men have the same rights and that there is no truth in the state. But this equality of principle remains nominal; at decisive moments the government continues to be violent and the majority of men remain objects of history. Marxism seeks to destroy the alternative of subjective or objective politics by submitting history neither to the arbitrary will of certain men nor to the exigencies of an ungraspable World Spirit, but to the exigencies of a certain condition considered human by all men, namely, the condition of the proletariat.

Despite so many inaccurate accounts, Marxism does not subject men to the will of the proletariat or the Party considered as a sum of individuals, justifying this new despotism as best it can with a mystical predestination according to the traditional recipes of violence. If it accords a privilege to the proletariat it does so because on the basis of the internal logic of its condition, and its least settled mode of existence—that is, apart from any messianic illusion—the proletarians "who are not gods" are the only ones in a position to realize humanity. It recognizes a mission in the proletariat—not a providential one but an historical one and that means that the proletariat, if we take its role in the given historical constellation, moves toward the recognition of man by man. Violence, deception, terror, compromise, finally the subjectivity of the leaders and the Party, which runs the risk of transforming other men into objects, find their limit in that they are involved in the service of a human society, namely, proletarian society, which is indivisibly a network of human will and economic fact, and more profound than all that, in the disturbing idea of true coexistence to which it has only to lend its voice and vocabulary.

Marxists have thoroughly criticized abstract humanism for wishing to pass directly to the classless society or, rather, postulating it. They did so only in the name of a concrete universality which is that of the proletarians of every country already being prepared in the present. The Bolsheviks may have insisted upon the role of the Party in the Revolution; they may have rejected the social-democratic notion of a revolution by parliamentary means as too naive (and too cunning), but they did not wish to surrender the revolution to alternations of enthusiasm and despair on the part of the unorganized masses. Although the actions of the Bolsheviks cannot at every moment reflect the immediate sentiments of the proletariat, they must on balance and in the world as a whole hasten the advancement of the proletariat and continuously raise the consciousness of the proletariat's condition because it is the initiation of truly human coexistence. There is a great deal of mistrust among Marxists, but at the same time a fundamental confidence in the spontaneity of history. "The masses sensed what we were unable to formulate consciously," says Lenin in his speech before the Fourth Congress of the Communist International. For a Marxist, the sense of the masses is always true, not that they always have a clear idea of the revolution throughout the world, but because they have the "instinct" for it, as its moving force, and because better than anyone else they know their capacity for the undertaking which itself is an essential element of the historical situation. The proletariat and the Party machine regulate one another, not in the style of demagoguery which would not annul the apparatus of absolute centralism because this would paralyze the masses, but through the vital communication of the masses with *their* Party, or the interaction of history in the making with the idea of history.

The Marxist theory of the proletariat is not an appendix or an addendum. It is truly the core of the doctrine because it is in the condition of the proletariat that abstract concepts come to life and life itself becomes awareness. Marxists have often compared revolutionary violence to the doctor's intervention at a birth. This implies that the new society is already in existence and that violence is justified, not by remote goals, but by the vital needs of a new humanity already in view. It is the theory of the proletariat which makes Marxist politics absolutely distinct from all other authoritarian politics and makes the frequent formal analogies between them superficial. If we wish to understand Marxist violence and to grasp communism as it is today we must go back over the theory of the proletariat. In the name of the proletariat, Marx describes a situation such that those in it, and they alone, have the *full experience* of the freedom and universality which Marx considered the defining characteristics of man. The development of production, says Marx, created a *world market,* i.e., an economy in which every man depends for his life on what happens everywhere else in the world. Most men and even some of the proletariat only experience this relation to the rest of the world as a fate and draw from it only resignation.

> The social power, i.e., the multiplied productive force, which arises through the cooperation of different individuals as it is determined by the division of labour, appears to these individuals, since their cooperation is not voluntary but has come about naturally, not as their own united power, but as an alien force existing outside of them, the origin and goal of which they are ignorant, which they thus cannot control, which on the contrary passes through a peculiar series of phases and stages independent of the will and the action of man, may even be the prime governor of these.[10]

Insofar as the proletarian experiences this dependency at work and as it affects wages, he more than anyone else has a chance of experiencing it as an "alienation" or an "externalization"; insofar as destiny fixes upon him more than anyone else, he is best placed for taking his life into his hands and creating his own fate out of it rather than merely bearing it. "The community of revolutionary proletarians, on the other hand . . . take their conditions of existence and those of all members of society under their control . . . conditions which were previously abandoned to chance and had won an independent existence against the separate individuals . . . and through their separation had become a bond alien to them."[11]

[10] K. Marx and F. Engels, *The German Ideology*, Moscow, Progress Publishers, 1964, p. 46.
[11] *Ibid.*, p. 92.

Thus there is an objective premise underlying the Revolution, namely the existence of universal dependence, and a subjective premise, which is the consciousness of such dependency as alienation. One can see the very particular relation between these two premises. They cannot be added to one another: it is not a matter of there being *both* an objective proletarian condition and an awareness of its condition which might be added to it gratuitously. The "objective" condition itself induces the proletarian to become conscious of his condition, the very act of living that way motivates the awakening of consciousness. It is the proletarian's condition that leads him to the point of detachment and freedom at which it is possible to be conscious of dependency. For the proletarian individuality or self-consciousness and class consciousness are absolutely identical.

A nobleman always remains a nobleman, a commoner always a commoner, apart from his other relationships, a quality inseparable from his individuality. The division between the personal and the class individual, the accidental nature of the conditions of life for the individual appears only with the emergence of the class, which is itself a product of the bourgeoisie. . . . For the proletarians, on the other hand, the condition of their existence, labour, and with it all the conditions of existence governing modern society, have become something accidental, something over which they, as separate individuals, have no control, and over which no *social* organization can give them control.[12]

In reflection every man can *conceive* of himself as simply a man and thereby rejoin the others. But that is through an

[12] *Ibid.*, pp. 93–94.

abstraction: he has to forget his peculiar circumstances, and, once he has gone back from thought to living, he again conducts himself as a Frenchman, a doctor, a bourgeois, etc. Universality is only conceived, it is not lived. By contrast, the condition of the proletarian is such that he can detach himself from special circumstances not just in thought and by means of an abstraction but in reality and through the very process of his life. He alone *is* the universality that he reflects upon; he alone achieves the self-consciousness that the philosophers have anticipated. With the proletariat history transcends the particularities of provincialism and chauvinism and *"finally has put world-historical, empirically universal individuals in place of local ones."*[13] The proletariat has not received its *historical mission* from an unfathomable World Spirit; it is this world spirit manifestly since it inaugurates universality and human concord. Hegel distinguished in society the substantial class (the peasants), the thinking class (workers and producers), and the universal class (the State functionaries). But the Hegelian State is only universal *de jure,* or because the functionaries (Hegel himself and History as they conceive it) confer on it this status and value. The proletariat is universal *de facto,* or manifestly in its very condition of life. It achieves what is universally valuable because it alone is above particularities, it alone is in a universal condition. The proletariat is no sum of wills each choosing the Revolution on their own behalf, nor yet an objective force like gravity or universal attraction; it is the sole authentic intersubjectivity because it alone lives

13 *Ibid.,* p. 46, our emphasis.

simultaneously the separation and union of individuals. Of course, the pure proletariat is a limit-case:

> Capitalism would not be capitalism if the proletariat *pur sang* were not surrounded by a large number of exceedingly motley types intermediate between the proletariat and the semi-proletarian . . . between the semi-proletarian and the small peasant . . . between the small peasant and the middle peasant, and so on, and if the proletariat itself were not divided into more developed and less developed strata, if it were not divided according to territorial origin, trade, sometimes according to religion, and so on.[14]

It is because of this that there is need for a Party which clarifies the proletariat to itself, for a Party of iron, as Lenin said. This, too, is the source of the violent intervention of subjectivity in history. But the intervention, according to Marxism, would lose its meaning if it were not exercised according to the pattern outlined by history itself, unless the Party's activity were not the prolongation and fulfillment of the spontaneous existence of the proletariat.

We began with abstract alternatives: either history is made spontaneously or else it is the leaders who make it through cunning and strategy—either one respects the freedom of the proletarians and the revolution is a chimera or else one judges for them what they want and the Revolution becomes Terror. In practice Marxism goes beyond these alternatives: approximation, compromise, Terror are inevitable, since history is contingent. But there is a limit to them inasmuch as within this contingency certain vectors are

14 Lenin, *Left-Wing Communism—An Infantile Disorder, loc. cit.*, p. 74.

traceable and outline a rational order in the proletarian community. It may well prove necessary to yield to an inimical course of events, but under pain of losing its meaning, compromise can only be practiced "in order to *raise*— not lower—the general level of proletarian class-consciousness, revolutionary spirit, and ability to fight and win."[15] The same thing might be said of Terror which by contrast, forces history's hand. The theory of the proletariat as the vehicle of history's meaning is the humanist face of Marxism. It is a Marxist principle that the Party and its leaders should translate into words and ideas what is implicit in the practice of the proletariat. The revolutionary leadership may appeal from the existing proletariat, blinded by the agencies of distraction, to the "pure" proletariat of which we have given a theoretical schema, or from the "decomposed" proletariat to the "honest elements of the proletariat." Occasionally, it pushes the proletariat forward. Conversely, it may have to restrain them, it being the work of geometrical minds—and of provocateurs—to encourage communism to march straight ahead. The general principles of communism have to be applied "*to the specific features* in the objective development towards communism, which are different in each country and which we must be above to discover, study and predict."[16] Local and contemporary history are not sciences and cannot be treated on the level of "universal history." Furthermore, the contact broken between the spontaneous life of the masses and the exigencies of a proletarian victory planned by the leaders should be re-established after

[15] *Ibid.*
[16] *Ibid.*, p. 89.

some foreseeable interruption and within a man's lifetime. Otherwise the proletarian will not see for what he is sacrificing himself and we shall have returned to the Hegelian philosophy of the State: a few functionaries of History who possess knowledge for all and carry out the will of the World Spirit with the blood of others. Local history must have a patent connection with universal history without which the proletariat lapses into the provincialism it should have transcended.

The theory of the proletariat gives a general orientation to the Marxist dialectic which distinguishes it from the dialectic in the sophists and skeptics. The skeptic relishes the thought that every idea turns into its opposite, that "everything is relative," that, from one aspect, large is small and small large, that religion which comes from the heart turns into an inquisition, violence, hypocrisy, and thus irreligion, that the freedom and virtue of the eighteenth century, once on the side of the government become enforced freedom and forced virtue, the law of suspects, Terror and thus sanctimonious hypocrisy. Kant produces Robespierre. The Marxist dialectic is not intended to add another chapter to history's ironies: it means to put an end to them. Granted, our intentions are transformed once we turn them to action; granted, too, that there are agitators and that what seemed in the spirit of the Revolution may in the actual moment become a reactionary maneuver; yes, "the entire history of Bolshevism, both before and after the October Revolution is *full* of instances of changes of tack, conciliatory tactics and compromises with other parties, including bourgeois parties!"[17] Yes,

[17] *Ibid.*, p. 70.

"it is folly, not revolutionism, to deprive ourselves in advance of any freedom of action, openly to inform any enemy who is at present better armed than we are whether we shall fight him and when. To accept battle at a time when it is obviously advantageous to the enemy, but not to us, is criminal; political leaders of the revolutionary class are absolutely useless if they are incapable of 'changing tack, or offering conciliation and compromise' in order to take evasive action in a patently disadvantageous battle."[18] So there are detours. But *Marxist Machiavellianism differs from pure Machiavellianism inasmuch as it transforms compromise through awareness of compromise, alters the ambiguity of history through awareness of ambiguity, and it makes detours consciously—calling them detours. Marxism calls a retreat a retreat and it places the details of local politics and tactical paradoxes in the larger perspective.*

The Marxist dialectic subordinates tactical deviations at a particular moment to a general definition of the phase concerned and makes that definition known. Thus it does not allow just anything to be anything. In every case it is known where one is going and why. A dialectical world is a world on the move where every idea communicates with all others and where values can be reversed. All the same, it is not a bewitched world where ideas operate without any rule, where at any moment angels become devils and allies friends. Within a given period of history and a given policy of the Party, values are decided upon and are strictly adhered to because they arise out of the logic of history. It is this absolute within a surrounding contingency which consti-

18 *Ibid.,* p. 77.

tutes the difference between the Marxist dialectic and vulgar relativism. Lenin's speech before the Fourth Congress of International Communism[19] quoted above, offers a fine example of this policy of flexibility and frankness, unafraid of compromise because it dominates it. It concerns the justification of NEP. Lenin begins by describing the 1921 crisis. The peasant insurrections, he says, "before 1921 were, so to speak, a common occurrence in Russia." These insurrections had to be understood: "the masses sensed what we ourselves were not then able to formulate consciously but we admitted soon after, a few weeks later, namely, that the direct transition to purely socialist forms, to purely socialist distribution, was beyond our available strength." It was therefore necessary, for the moment, to pursue objectives short of socialism[20] and this is why Lenin does not hesitate to speak of a "retreat." The first step on the new road was the stabilization of the ruble which he thought was almost accomplished within a year. With this as a base, he believes he can offer assurance that the discontent among the peasants has ceased to be serious or widespread.[21] Small-scale industry is improving. The situation is not as good in heavy industry. From 1921 to 1922 it is possible to speak only of a slight improvement. But the question is a vital one: "If we

19 Report to the Fourth Congress of the Communist International, November 13, 1922; Coll. works, Vol. 33 (Translator).

20 ". . . although it is not a socialist form, state capitalism would be for us, and for Russia, a more favorable form than the existing one."

21 "The peasantry may be dissatisfied with one aspect or another of the work of our authorities. They may complain about this. That is possible, of course, and inevitable, because our machinery of state and our state-operated economy are still too inefficient to avert it; but any serious dissatisfaction with us on the part of the peasantry as a whole is quite out of the question.

fail to preserve and build up heavy industry, then without it
we are simply lost as an independent State." We should have
foreign loans but they are refused to us. We are alone. We
can only rely upon the resources of our own trade. They are
being employed to reconstruct heavy industry. We are setting up mixed companies in which a fraction of the capital
belongs to private capitalists abroad.

> We already have proof that, as a state, we are able to trade . . .
> and we have realized that we still have much to learn. . . . I
> have said that we have done a host of foolish things, . . . four
> enemies blame us and say that Lenin himself admits that the
> Bolsheviks have done a host of foolish things, I want to reply
> to this: yes, but you know, the foolish things we have done are
> nonetheless very different from yours. We have only just be-
> gun to learn, but we are learning so methodically that we are
> certain to achieve good results.

Both Russians and foreigners must learn. The resolution of
the 1921 Party Congress is too Russian. We have to explain
it to the foreigners and they must learn from us the nature
of revolutionary action. As for ourselves, we must learn to
study to understand what we have studied.

Rarely has a chief of government been seen to admit so
frankly the discontent of the masses, to provide reasons for
the discontent and upon it to construct a new policy, himself pointing out the risks of failure, recognizing his mistakes, schooling himself with the masses, with foreigners,
and with the facts. It is easy to see Lenin has no fear of
"giving weapons to the reactionaries." He does not ignore
the use that might be made of his words. Nevertheless he
believes that speaking openly brings in more than it costs

because it associates the government with its subjects, and by giving it the support of the masses throughout the world it reconciles it with what for Marxism is the principal agent of history. It is no accident, nor, I suppose, out of any romantic disposition that the first newspaper of the U.S.S.R. was given the name Pravda. The cause of the proletariat is so universal that it can tolerate truth better than any other. What gives Lenin this freedom of tone, this simplicity and audacity, what saves him from intellectual panic and terrorism is his confidence, at the very moment where detours seem necessary, in history as the growth and emergence of the proletariat. What preserves the rational character of the Marxist dialectic is that in a given phase of the growth of the masses things have a name and only one name.[22]

It is the theory of the proletariat which radically distinguishes Marxism from every so-called "totalitarian" ideology. Of course, the idea of totality plays an essential role in Marxist thought. It is the concept of totality which underlies the whole Marxist critique of the "formal," "analytic,"

---

[22] It may be replied that this openminded policy with its frankness and reasonableness belongs to the spirit of 1917 or to the time of NEP but now belongs to lost illusions, recent experience having taught the Communists that one cannot fight without masks nor worry over the consciousness of the masses. This is a possibility, and indeed it seems to us that today's communism is characterized by a reduced emphasis on subjective conditions and mass consciousness—or, what comes to the same, by an increased emphasis upon the direction and consciousness of the leadership—all this having been made possible by the regime of generalized compromise to which the U.S.S.R. has been reduced since the failure of the revolution in Germany. However—we shall return to this later—the question is then to know whether the struggle is still a Marxist struggle, whether we are not witnessing a separation of the subjective and objective factors that Marx wished to unite in his conception of history, in other words, whether we still have the slightest reason to believe in a logic of history at a time when it is throwing overboard its dialectical rudder—the world proletariat.

and pseudo-objective nature of bourgeois thought. Marxism shows that a politics based upon man in general, the citizen in general, justice and truth in general, once it is inserted into the concrete totality of history, works to the advantage of very particular interests and it focuses its criticism on these relationships. In the same way it shows that the custom of separating problems (economic, political, philosophical, religious, etc.), like the principle of the separation of powers, veils their relation, convergence, and mutual significance in living history and thus retards the emergence of revolutionary consciousness.

The opponents of Marxism never fail to compare this "totalitarian" method with the Fascist ideology which also pretends to go from the formal to the actual, from the contractual to the organic. But the comparison is in bad faith. For fascism is nothing but a mimicry of Bolshevism. A single Party, propaganda, the justice of the state, the truth of the state—fascism retains everything of Bolshevism except what is essential, namely, the theory of the proletariat. For if the proletariat is the force on which revolutionary society is based and if the proletariat is that "universal class" we have described from Marx, then the interests of this class bring human values into history and the proletariat's power is the power of humanity. Fascist violence, by contrast, is not the violence of a universal class, it is the violence of a "race" or late-starting nation; it does not follow the course of things, but pushes against them.

However, it is no accident that formal analogies can be found between fascism and Bolshevism; the *raison d'être* of fascism as fear of revolution is to institute change while trying to confiscate for itself the energies freed by the decomposition of liberalism. In order to play its role as a distracting force it is therefore necessary that fascism formally resemble Bolshevism. The only striking difference is in the content—but there it is immense: the propaganda, which in Bolshevism is the means of proletarian intervention in the state and history, under fascism becomes the art of making the masses accept a military state. The Party, which under Bolshevism focuses the spontaneous movement of the masses upon a genuine universality, under fascism becomes the efficient cause behind every movement of the masses and turns them toward the traditional goals of a military state. Therefore it cannot be overemphasized that Marxism only criticizes formal thought to the benefit of proletarian thought which will be more capable than the latter of achieving "objectivity," "truth," and "universality," in other words, of realizing the values of liberalism. It is in this way that the meaning and measure of Marxist "realism" is given. Revolutionary action does not aim at ideas or values, it aims at the power of the proletariat. But the proletarian by his mode of existence, and as a "man of universal history" is the inheritor of liberal humanism. The result is that revolutionary action does not *replace* the service of ideas with service of a class: it identifies the two. Marxism in principle denies any conflict between the exigencies of realism and those of ethics since the so-called "ethics" of capitalism is a mystification, and the power of the proletariat is in reality what the bourgeois apparatus is only nominally. Marxism is no immorality but rather the determination not to consider virtues and ethics only in the heart of each man but also in the coexistence of men. The alternative posed between the actual and the ideal is transcended in the concept of the proletariat as the concrete vehicle of values.

It is also through the historical activity of the proletariat that Marxism resolves the famous problem of ends and means. Since the publication of *Darkness at Noon* there is not an educated man in the Anglo-Saxon world or in France who is not in agreement with the goals of the Marxist revolution, regretting only that Marxism should pursue such noble ends through such ignoble methods. Actually, Marxism has nothing in common with the joyful cynicism of "at all costs." First of all, it should be observed that the categories of "ends" and "means" are entirely alien to Marxism. An end is a result to come which one proposes for oneself and seeks to realize. It ought to be superfluous to recall that Marxism very consciously distinguishes itself from utopianism by defining revolutionary action not as the adoption of a certain number of ends through reasoning and will, but as the simple extrapolation of a *praxis* already at work in history, of a reality that is already committed, namely, the proletariat. It is not a question of representing a "society of the future." Rather than the awareness of a goal, there is the espousal of an impossibility, in which the present world is grasped in contradiction and decomposition; rather than the fantastic conception of a paradise on earth, there is the patient analysis of past and present history as a class struggle; and finally there is the creative decision to pass beyond this chaos through the universal class which will relay the foundations of human history. Revolutionary action can acquire a perspective by drawing out the lines of proletarian devel-opment into the future. But Marxists patently refuse to as-sume "ends"; none of them, says Lenin, can "promise" the last phase of communism—because one can only validly think what one has in some way lived, the rest being noth-ing but imagination. Now precisely because it does not have the resort and pious excuse of "ends" Marxism is unable to acknowledge "any and all means." Because it abstains from describing a heavenly future and from justifying its daily deeds in terms of it, Marxism must distinguish itself through a socialist style which it does as proletarian action, extrapo-lating, specifying, and redirecting the spontaneous *praxis* of the proletariat along its proper path. In so doing it will not observe the formal and "universal" rules of sincerity and objectivity because these are the rules of the capitalist game and to treat a person as an end who treats others as a means is likewise to treat them as means.

But Marxism acquires an ethics without seeking it insofar as it is proletarian action because the proletariat, from the standpoint of the Marxist conception of history, is not an elementary force that one serves for the sake of ends that transcend it, but a force polarized toward certain values by the very logic of the situation which it encounters. The pro-letariat is both an objective factor of political economy and a system of subjective awareness, or rather a style of coex-istence at once fact and value, in which the logic of history joins the forces of labor and the authentic experience of human life. Consequently, the categories of value and utility are suffused in the proletariat, which is not to say that utility is the standard of value (as with the Commissar), nor value the measure of utility (as for the Yogi), but because proletarian utility is value as it is effective in history. Proletarian action involves as much humanity as is possible in a decaying society and it is the least driven to deceit because it has the most ties in contemporary society and from all sides unites the forces working for the overthrow of the bourgeois machine. The Marxist does not live with his eyes fixed on a transcendent future, forgiving deplorable tactics in the name of ultimate ends and absolving himself on account of his good intentions; he is the only one who denies himself such recourse.

In his discussion of contemporary problems Trotsky could —as we have acknowledged here—fall into contradiction with his own principles of government. All the same, as a theoretician he expresses an essential notion of Marxism when he speaks of a "dialectic interdependence between means and ends."[23] In a viable Marxism these two notions are "relativized," end and means being reversible because the means is nothing but the end—the power of the proletariat—in its historical form. In reality, it is not a case of there being an end *and* the means; there are only means or ends, however one wants to put it, or in other words there is a revolutionary process in which every moment is equally indispensable and thus just as valuable as any utopian "final" moment. "Dialectic materialism does not know dualism between means and end. The end flows naturally from the historical movement. Organically the means are subordinated to the end. . . . Seeds of wheat must be sown in order

23 "Their Morals and Ours," in *The Basic Writings of Trotsky, loc. cit.,* p. 397.

to yield an ear of wheat."[24] Marxism rejects the option between Machiavellianism and an ethical standpoint, between the viewpoints of "at all costs" and the "let justice be done though the heavens may fall." It does so because he who acts morally becomes immoral as soon as he loses regard for the nature of his acts, and victory is defeat wherever it is not the success of a new humanity. There is no question of reaching the goal by means that are not in character with it. For the revolutionary party there is no question of there being any conflict between its *raison d'être* and its surrounding conditions, *since, apart from accidents, history involves a logic of a sort in which it is impossible for nonproletarian means to achieve proletarian ends.* For history, despite its detours, its cruelties, and its ironies already contains a working logic in the condition of the proletariat which solicits the contingency of events and the freedom of individuals and so draws them toward reason.

In its essence Marxism is the idea that history has a meaning—in other words, that it is intelligible and has a direction—that it is moving toward the power of the proletariat, which as the essential factor of production is capable of resolving the contradictions of capitalism, of organizing a humane appropriation of nature, and, as the "universal class," able to transcend national and social conflicts as well

[24] *Ibid.,* pp. 396–397. It is difficult to see why in a recent interview André Breton attributes to Trotsky the famous precept "the end justifies the means" which, on the contrary, Trotsky rejected in his question "If the end justifies the means what then justifies the end?" The truth is that Trotsky, like all Marxists, rejects all politics in terms of ends or good intentions because it is a mystification in a world so far devoted to violence and also because it retards revolutionary action. If André Breton abandoned Trotsky from this very moment to join with the partisans of "pure means," not much can be left of his Marxism.

as the struggle between man and man. To be a Marxist is to believe that economic problems and cultural or human problems are a single problem and that the proletariat as history has shaped it holds the solution to that problem. In modern language, it is to believe that history has a *Gestalt,* in the sense German writers give to the word, a holistic system moving toward a state of equilibrium, the classless society which cannot be achieved without individual effort and action, but which is outlined in the present crisis as their solution—the power of man over nature and the mutual reconciliation of men. In music a given note on the strings requires a note of the same pitch from the wind and brass; in an organism a given state of the respiratory system requires a given state of the cardiovascular or sympathetic nervous system; in an electric conductor of a certain design the charge at a given point must be such that the whole obeys a fixed law of distribution. In the same way, history, according to Marxist politics, is a system which proceeds by ups and downs toward proletarian power and the development of a world proletariat as the norm of history calls for determinate solutions in specific areas, each partial chance observing its implications for the whole. For example, the proletarian seizure of the economic apparatus, the proletarian invasion of the bourgeois state and an internationalist ideology are, for Marxists, concordant phenomena and so closely linked that it is impossible to conceive a prolonged neglect of one of them that would not in the end affect all of them and alter the general development of the Revolution. Of course, each of the three Marxist themes of mass spontaneity, internationalism, and the construction of an economic infrastructure may, according to circumstances and tactical necessities, be emphasized at the expense of the others, and revolutionary action may stress now one point and now another. The world development of the proletariat may demand that the needs of a national proletariat be sacrificed for a time to the progress of the whole movement. But with all the detours, with all the compromises, with all the conflicts en route, with all the imbalance one likes to imagine, a Marxist conception of history aims at the convergence of at least the main line of events upon the development of proletarian consciousness and power. One hundred years after the *Communist Manifesto* and thirty years after the first proletarian Revolution, how do things stand in this regard?

*   *   *

The proletarian Revolution was made in a country where the proletariat did not have access to a modern industrial economy. This was so much out of line that the Party itself and its leaders decided only hesitantly to "mount" the democratic stage of the process. In itself this fact is no refutation of Marxism: the backward state of Russia in 1916 upon reflection appeared to be a factor in favor of the Revolution, provided one observes that the Marxist ideology, which had been developed in contact with a Western economy, stood to acquire from a new proletariat, which had been subject to quasi-colonial exploitation, a surplus of explosive energy. This reverse action of an advanced ideology and technology upon a backward country does not destroy the dialectical framework. It is the pre-1917 Marxists who were thinking abstractly when they overlooked lateral interaction and im-

agined parallel developments in every country of the world.
At any rate, the birth of the Revolution in Russia, with all
the consequences that flow from it, profoundly modifies the
equilibrium of subjective and objective factors in the revolutionary process.

In Russia, consciousness was more advanced than the
economy and the proletariat had to provide itself with an
economy in line with its ideology. If one recalls that in Marx
a society's mode of production—its relation to nature which
it transforms—and the social relations of men in that society
are only two aspects of the same phenomenon, there could
be no question as long as Russia had not received the economic apparatus it needed of establishing "socialist" relations
between men there. The result was, after the vague attempts
of War Communism, the paradox of NEP, that is to say, a
socialist revolution which rallied behind "a non-socialist element, namely State capitalism."[25] Russian socialism sought
in this way to strengthen its foundations, to put itself in step
with the spontaneous movement of history which it had first
forestalled. One might say that it was "waiting" for the
economy. Could it have continued in this path without destroying itself? The answer must be in the negative, since
after Lenin's death even the left (which always tried to
ground its action in a general conception of history) established a program of industrialization designed to hasten the
achievement of socialism. On this occasion it was no longer
socialist ideology "waiting" for the economy but rather the
latter which had to catch up with socialist ideology. It was
Trotsky's argument that this unprecedented effort could be

[25] Lenin, report to the Fourth Congress of the Communist International, *loc. cit.*

accomplished solely in the name of socialist forces and the proletarian ideology—spontaneity of the masses and internationalism—could by anticipation inspire the construction of a modern economy of which, in classical Marxism it is the ultimate expression and crown. This was Trotsky's message when he demanded that the task of industrialization and collectivization should rest upon a "workers' democracy" which would control the economy and restore initiative to the masses. According to him, it was necessary during this critical period, which might last for years, to stake everything on mass consciousness and its revolutionary will and to put the proletarian consciousness described by Marx at the helm of an economy still unable to support it. Yet Trotsky himself, in other areas, had made very strong arguments against a rigid proletarian politics. In 1929, for example, against the extreme left he defended the principle of Russian concessions in China[26] because, as he said, Russia is the homeland of the Revolution. This was an admission that in the conflict of imperialist countries the best means of defending the Chinese proletariat lay not in claiming its direct and complete control over Chinese territories and that the presence of the Red Army might be a better guarantee of the Chinese proletariat's future than a Chinese commune easily overthrown by the imperialists.

But if the Marxist principle of internationalism can admit such variations why should the spontaneity of the masses remain a rigid principle? If the fact (in itself regrettable) of a revolution in a single country confers upon it a special role in the dynamics of the international class struggle, allowing

26 *La Défense de l'U.R.S.S. et l'Opposition, loc. cit.*

it to condemn the "abstraction" of a politics seeking to respect the will of each national proletariat and in the end to
"overstep" the Chinese proletariat should the necessity arise,
why should not the historical conditions experienced by the
Soviet Union—its historical backwardness, its isolation, the
threat of war, the necessity of a quick victory, the fatigue of
the masses of ten years of revolution—have permitted "over-
stepping" the proletarian consciousness, i.e., resorting to
nonsocialist forces and condemning the abstraction of a
"workers' democracy," in this instance as well?

The moment one begins to think concretely, i.e., to take
account in any political decision not only of working class
consciousness but also of the economic and military ap-
paratuses—the objective factors working in their favor and
representing them in day to day history—working class consciousness as such can no longer provide the standard of
what is revolutionary and what is not. The Russian Revolution might have followed the strict line of proletarian politics if it had spread throughout Europe, if other countries
had provided the Soviet economy with the credits it needed
and had come to relieve the Russian advance guard at the
post it had held since 1917. But nothing of the sort happened. Trotsky himself wrote that the revolutionary ebb was
"unavoidable under given historical conditions" and that
there was no recipe for preserving "revolutionary power
under the condition of world counterrevolution."[27] This
amounts to saying that *the permanent revolution is impossible at the very moment that it becomes necessary*. Again
Lenin defined socialism as "the power of the soviets plus

[27] "Their Morals and Ours," *loc. cit.*, p. 382.

electrification." But what happens if the world revolution stagnates—with all its consequences, the threat of war abroad, the curtailment of political action—and these two principles become dissociated?

What happens if the spontaneity of the masses, the resort to proletarian forces, on one side, and, on the other, industrialization and the development of a modern economy at a time when the world proletariat is weak and the Russian proletariat exhausted and isolated—what if all these cease to be complementary objectives, as Marx and Lenin believed, and become distinct and even alternative tasks? Of the three fundamental principles brought to light in a proletarian philosophy of history—spontaneity of the masses, internationalism and the construction of an economic infrastructure—the first principle became foremost and the other two dropped into the background since the actual course of history permitted revolution in only one country and one that was not equipped for it?

Marxism had conceived the Revolution as the product of a combination of objective and subjective factors. If not in theory, which remains unchanged, in revolutionary practice, at least, the present historical phase ruptures the equilibrium of these two factors. In comparison with the classical vision, it overemphasizes the objective factor of the economic infrastructure at the expense of the working class consciousness. At present the revolution relies less upon the development of a national and world proletariat than the clairvoyance of the Party, the effectiveness of its plans and the discipline of the workers. It has become an almost purely voluntary enterprise. As far as the Party is concerned it is no longer a matter of discerning the thrust of the Revolution in Russia and elsewhere in the world, or of deciphering history as it is made, or following up its spontaneous course. Since history did not bring the 1917 Revolution the support it expected, it was necessary to force the march of history and do violence to it. On the international scene, the result was a politics of prudence which restrained the thrust of national proletariats and admitted class cooperation. In Russia itself the result was a program of forced industrialization and collectivization which where necessary appealed to the profit motive and did not shrink from instituting privilege and liquidating the illusions of 1917. Finally, this was also the source of the paradox of the Terror twenty years after the Revolution.

It therefore becomes possible, on the basis of facts that as far as we can establish are correct, to construct a picture of Soviet life which is the opposite of proletarian humanism.[28] The revolutionary significance of the present policy is hidden beneath the "economic infrastructure" of the regime and will only appear later, like those seeds deep in the earth which germinate after centuries. It is not detectable in this policy itself and can only be discerned if one approaches the present from a Marxist framework. That is why the classical teachings survive. But the contemporary deviations make reconciliation difficult. The picture of Soviet life that we ourselves are able to construct resembles one of those ambiguous figures that can be either a flat mosaic or a cube in space according to the angle of view, though neither of these

[28] This is what Koestler does in *The Yogi and the Commissar*, and other Essays, London, Jonathan Cape, 1945.

interpretations rests on the object itself. For example, in the technical field of political economy Russian socialists occasionally try to formulate and plan optimum results. (Leontiev, for example, has formulated the thesis of the persistence of value in the present transitional period.)[29] But one notices no position at all taken with respect to the essential point of the relation between objective and subjective factors. This is not without reason. For an "objectivist" theory of the present phase, which would temporarily push aside the subjective factors of history and ideology, would not be a Marxist theory: it would strike at the central thesis of Marxism, namely, the identity of the subjective and objective factors. For the most part, one has to make do with a sort of shuffle between theoretical Marxism and the policy imposed by history, with the Communists replying to questions about the U.S.S.R. with texts from Marx and with a critique of Marxology and a defense of living Marxism when confronted with texts from Marx. The objectivists' political education leads them to assume a Marxist horizon and a classless society and so they perceive measures that an uneducated observer would instinctively consider reactionary as detours in the direction of a socialist future. In the present phase the relation between the present and the future or between eco-

29 This effort, in the beginning at least, was officially encouraged. Thus there is no reason to believe that the Party leadership in principle rules out the theoretical elaboration and revision of viewpoints. The only reason to doubt it is that revisionism has often been a veiled capitulation. If there are few attempts to come to the point and think through the Soviet situation, whether on the level of economics or philosophy, it is very much because it is difficult to theorize on a situation in which historical contingencies predominate and upset rational forecasts. Of course, in this respect bourgeois political economy is in no better position.

nomic development and the proletarian standpoint has become too complex and too indirect for anyone to formulate; it is on the order of the occult. The actual state of affairs is revisionist; today's Communists are unlike those of yesterday, they have fewer illusions, they are working for a more distant result, they expect all sorts of mediations. But there is a hesitancy in formulating this revisionism expressly because it would throw in question the harmony of the proletarian ideology with economic development, in other words, the human significance and value of communism.

If certain American calculations[30] can be trusted, the classical role of the proletariat within the Bolshevik Party has steadily declined. At the 17th Party Congress (1934), 80 per cent of the delegates were old Communists who had joined before 1919. At the 18th Congress (1939) they numbered 14.8 per cent. At the 17th Congress 9.3 per cent of delegates were manual workers. The 18th Congress does not give statistics on the social origins of the delegates and the Party statutes must have been changed so as to eliminate the sections concerning the social background of members. At the same time a new form of social differentiation emerged. In June, 1931, four years after the initiation of the first Five-Year Plan, Stalin in a speech gave the order to eliminate the equality of pay. Henceforth the motive of socialist emulation was to be reinforced with the nonsocialist profit motive. In 1936,

---

[30] Given by Koestler, *The Yogi and the Commissar*, pp. 179–180. Unfortunately we cannot check the sources. Koestler takes his figures from Solomon M. Schwartz, "Heads of Russian Factories," *Social Research*, Vol. IX, No. 3 (September 1942), pp. 315–333, who claims to reproduce official figures from the Mandate Commission of the 17th and 18th Party Congresses (p. 330).

at a mine in the Donetz[31] Basin, 60 employees were earning 1,000 to 2,500 rubles per month, 70 from 800 to 1,000 rubles per month, 400 were earning 500 to 800 rubles per month, and the remaining thousand workers were earning an average of 125 rubles per month. In the more important industries the salaries of the directors, chief engineers, and administrators were higher. It has not been possible to abide by Lenin's principle declared in *State and Revolution* that no member of the state apparatus would receive a larger salary than a qualified worker. Article 10 of the 1936 Constitution re-established the right to make a will and to inherit which had been abolished by the decree of 27 April, 1918. A decree of 2 October, 1940[32] fixed the annual pension payments at between 150 and 200 rubles for lower level teaching and between 300 and 500 rubles for higher level teaching. Until 1932, 65 per cent of the students in technical institutions had to come from unskilled working class families.[33] A decree of 19 September, 1932 tacitly abandoned the principle of the "Workers' Nucleus."[34] Special schools were established for the sons of officials.[35] There are scholarships for the children of poor families; they are given out to those students who have "excellent" in two-thirds of their examinations and "good" for the remaining third.

The repression of juvenile delinquency, abortion, taxing

31 *Trud*, 20 January, 1936 cited by Koestler, *The Yogi and the Commissar*, p. 162.

32 *Izvestia*, 3 October, 1940; cited by Koestler, *Ibid.*, p. 156.

33 *Pravda*, July 13, 1928, cited by Koestler, *loc. cit.*

34 Koestler, *loc. cit.*

35 Koestler, *ibid.*, p. 157, decree of August 23, 1943.

of bachelors, spinsters, and families with less than three children[36] are evidence that Soviet society has reimposed traditional norms. The official recognition of the Metropolitan Sergius as patriarch on September 12, 1943; pan-Slavic congresses held officially in Moscow since 1941; the presentation of Nevsky, Katuzov, and Suvorov as precursors in Stalin's speech on the twenty-fourth anniversary of the Revolution; finally, the replacement of the "people's commissars" by "Ministers"—all these details, whatever the necessity of tactical maneuvers to placate bourgeois allies, objectively have had the effect of restoring prerevolutionary ideologies and, in any case, mark a regression in the proletarian ideology.

Parallel with these developments, the Party is increasingly in control of political life and dictatorship increases its power. In 1922 the revolutionary-socialist plot in which two Bolsheviks were killed and Lenin wounded was not followed by any executions. Again in 1931 Ryutin, whose clandestine program was extremely violent, was not condemned to death. From 1934 to the outbreak of war, the distinction between political divergence and common law crimes was rescinded. Thus, at the same time that it shelves its external policy of working-class internationalism, the regime reduces the influence of the proletariat in internal politics and relies upon a new class whose mode of life is distinct from that of the masses and on occasions employs ideologies classically regarded as reactionary. From time to time the Communists say that they have been stripped of their "illusions." We would put this another way: they are for the moment unable to believe in that historical logic according to which the

[36] *Ibid.*, pp. 172–176.

construction of a socialist economy and the development of production rests upon working-class consciousness which it in turn reinforces. We are not saying that in the future the U.S.S.R. will possess a ruling class similar to that of capitalist countries, since the privileges in cash or kind are based upon effort and do not carry with them any right to exploit one's fellow men. We think it childish to explain contemporary developments in terms of a "lust for power" or the Party interests. We do say that the construction of the socialist framework of the economy has been at the expense of a regression in the proletarian ideology and that for reasons related to these trends—socialist revolution in a single country, revolutionary stagnation and historical corruption in the rest of the world—the U.S.S.R. is not the proletarian light of history Marx once described.

But it will be, it might be said. Perhaps. But once the generation in power, who were shaped by the classics and who practiced Marxist politics has been ousted because of age, where can we look for a corrective? Will the weight of those outside the Party not be decisive? The Communists say with good reason that men of honest intentions carry little weight in history where only deeds and their internal logic count for anything. Thus Stalin corrects the rightist deviations and Eisenstein's *Ivan the Terrible* is condemned, where it formerly won approval. But at the moment everything depends on the outlook of the leaders. Can one be sure that the new generation will be just as vigilant once the proletariat as the permanent source and counterbalance to Marxist politics is weakened inside and outside the U.S.S.R.? We are not saying that the U.S.S.R. could not otherwise survive. What we do ask is whether instead of a humane society open to the proletariat in every country of the world, we shall see a new type of society, which has yet to be studied, but in which one will not find the exemplary value of what Marx called the "classless society." There is all the more need for a study of Marxism and prerevolutionary ideologies in countries where the U.S.S.R. is the predominant influence. There is no doubt that in Rumania or in Yugoslavia the U.S.S.R. permits for the first time the serious raising of problems and their solution from which earlier regimes shrank. Contemporary communism is a mixed reality in which one encounters both "progressive" elements and bits from classical sociology, such as the cult of the leader. We are confronted with a new phenomenon. In the course of the proletariat's development, not only are there unexpected detours but the proletarian movement itself as a class conscious and spontaneous movement which transcends any utopian sociology has ceased to be the reference point of communist thought.

Lenin used to say that one should not view every event of local history from the perspective of universal history. The path which now seems to us tortuous with the passage of time may appear to have been the only possibility and *a fortiori* the shortest one once the whole story is told. Since the present writer does not have before him a completed history and is bound to a specific perspective—that of a French intellectual in 1946—his judgment may well be questioned. But the resort to a judgment based on the future is indistinguishable from the theological appeal to the Last Judgment, unless it is not simply a reversal of *pro* and *contra*, unless the future is in some sense outlined in the present, and unless hope is not simply faith and we know where we are going. One can always represent the inequality of salaries as a roundabout way toward equality—as "concrete" equality—or a nationalist policy as a detour on the way to internationalism—as "concrete" internationalism. It is only a question, it might be said, of an increased tension between the form and content, between the present and the future. But that amounts to saying that from now on the dialectic is undecipherable and that it is nothing but the transformation of opposites. Pierre Hervé says that Communist politics is "the daily elaboration of a strategy and tactic . . . adapted to the diverse conditions of time, place, situation, etc., and subordinate to the permanent interests of the workers."[37] For Lenin the fundamental law and condition of a valid compromise was "the elevation of the proletariat's general awareness, its revolutionary spirit and its capacity for struggle and victory."[38] In Hervé's opinion it is to "watch over the permanent interests of the workers." One can see that the criterion has changed. There has been a displacement from the subjective to the objective emphasis, from working class consciousness toward its permanent interest—toward the designs of the leaders, since from all evidence only the leaders possess the information necessary to determine the long-run interests of the workers.

Perhaps it was inevitable that this revision of Leninism should occur. But unlike the old politics the new one is incapable of harmonizing with the wishes of the proletariat. Perhaps there is still room for the dialectic, but it is from the

[37] *Action,* 15 February, 1946.
[38] Lenin, *Left-Wing Communism—An Infantile Disorder, loc. cit.*

standpoint of a God who comprehends Universal History. Anyone who adopts the perspective of his time, looking at it frankly and not through dreams and memories, sees only the process of constructing a collectivized economy. He does not see the proletariat wielding power as the "man of Universal History."

How is he to introduce into Party conduct the values which he holds as an individual? The proletariat as Marx conceived it embodied simultaneously the experience of individuality and universality. Today it has to choose between one or the other. To follow a broken dialectic the individual himself has to be broken. The result of this is—and here we return to matters of which we are more certain because we see them before our eyes—a kind of neo-Communism which borders on pragmatism. Every word we utter, a Communist told me, is not simply a word but an action as well. Therefore we should first ask ourselves not whether it is exact but whom it will profit. Marxists have always been concerned with the objective meaning of their discourse, but earlier they were able to believe that the course of events was on their side, which afforded them a degree of freedom. Truth was also a force. Autocriticism was and still is an official practice in the U.S.S.R. In France nowadays many Communists are distrustful of History and the consequences of what they say to the point where at bottom they hardly engage in discussion. In the end, arguing with you, one of them told me (it was over a philosophical problem), is already to have laid down one's arms. Ultimately, where history has no structure and no major trends it is no longer possible to *say* anything, since there are no periods, no lasting constellations and a thesis is only valid for the moment. We have left Plato's dialectical universe for the fluid universe of Heraclitus.

It is amusing to hear the same men attacking irrationalism who then practice it in their daily lives. When the Reverend Father Daniélou reproached the Communists for making tenders to the Catholics, P. Hervé replied that he is helpless against it because Father Daniélou himself, religion, and the Communist Party are all caught together in a dialectic which transcends them and controls political decisions. This is, to be sure, a Marxist response: religion has many aspects and it is the conjunction of world events which illuminates one aspect or another, according to the circumstances revealing its progressiveness or its reactionary nature. But even this can be understood in two ways. One may conclude that for a given period Marxists can make open alliances because they are in keeping with the direction of history at the moment. Or else it means that Marxists only make alliances subject to a mental reservation. In the first case Marxists are always sincere; in the latter case, they are never sincere. The former attitude is tied to a rational conception of history. Political romanticism is not a trait of those who wish to preserve Marxist humanism and the theory of the proletariat which is its foundation. It is not they who pose the alternatives of ethics or politics, deceit or failure. These heart-rending alternatives are the work of neo-Communism.

Confronted with the comparison between present-day Communism and its classical image, P. Hervé replies that "ancient communism exists only in the minds of historians. What does exist is a living communism which is what it is— and cannot regard itself as a deviation judged by historical

formulas."[39] All the same, if we are not to commit ourselves
to a Bergsonian flux, we ought to define a *concept* of communism, a method and style of Communist action, to know
by and large where we are going and why—for example,
communism is called communism. Communism only deserves its name (in the best sense of the word, which like
so many others has been distorted by the Nazis) if it ad-
vances toward community and communication, not toward
hierarchy.

Hervé reproaches us with "not recognizing Marxism at
the moment it begins to initiate political action . . . and
ceases to be simply a critique."[40] But then it is up to the
Communists to set the detours and compromises in a general
scheme, to set the details in a larger context, and to show
that communism is still communism, if not in a lifeless
identity, at least as a vital growth. Hervé speaks of "the
fascination aroused by the language and gestures of a by-
gone era." And he adds these words which hang heavily:
"There will never be another October 1917 . . ."[41] If he
means that the concrete circumstances of a revolution never
repeat themselves, that is evident. If, on the other hand, he
means that this revolution is not destined like that of 1917
to establish a new humanity, a new egalitarianism, a new
relation between men, then he is denying the very meaning
of Marxism and one can no longer see what he is fighting for.

Lenin, sitting on the steps of the tribunal, improvising the

[39] *Action*, 15 February, 1946.
[40] *Ibid.*
[41] *Ibid.*

reply he is about to make to a speaker; the simplicity, once in power, "camaraderie" in the finest sense of the word made the law of the state; social relations based on what men truly are rather than the prestige of money, power, and social influence; men taking their history into their own hands, commenting on events, facing up to it in common "resolutions," as the German Communists in Buchenwald still did after ten years in prison—if these are merely "illusions" that have been dropped completely, then one has abandoned the human meaning and *raison d'être* of communism. Given that human society is in a natural state of conflict, since every consciousness seeks to have its autonomy recognized by the others, Marx thought he had found the solution to the human problem in the proletariat insofar as it is detached from its natural surroundings, deprived of its private life and insofar as its fate is common to the proletariats of the world. The logic of the proletariat's situation was expected to lead it to join up with all other proletarians in a common struggle against their economic fate and its underlying forces in the creation of a *common freedom*. Just as inequalities of age, gifts, love, and diversity of individual backgrounds are transcended in a human couple in their life together and their common projects, so the diversity of working classes—the national, historical, and ethnic, peculiarities—should be transcended once the proletariat in every country recognizes itself in the others who face the same problems, the same enemy, and join in the same struggle against the same oppressive machinery. To say the very least, history has not taken this turn.

But it is one thing to recognize this fact, and quite another to declare Marxism outdated and look for a solution to the human problem along lines clearly shown to lead to eternal conflict. One does not get rid of Communist problems by showing that they are giving contemporary communism trouble. If, as we shall try to show, the essentials of the Marxist critique represent a definitive contribution to political consciousness and are superior to the Anglo-Saxon "trade union" ideology, the problems facing today's communism are also our problems. In no case do they legitimate our adoption of a hostile attitude toward communism, as though its critique of the present world loses all value because it does not find the historical hold and support it needed, or as though the impossibility of a solution suppresses the problem itself. What we must do with respect to communism is to define a practical stance of comprehension without adherence, of free study without disparagement, and to do what is in the power of each of us to avert a war in which everyone, whether he admits it or not, would choose in darkness and which would be a "dubious combat."

V. The Yogi and the Proletarian

WITH THE DECLINE of ideology and proletarian action there appears the real question with which Koestler struggles but never really formulates. Can the Revolution emerge from Terror? Does the proletariat have an historical mission which is simultaneously the dynamic force of the new society and the vehicle of human values? Or, on the contrary, is the Revolution inevitably an altogether arbitrary enterprise directed by leaders and a controlling group to which the rest submit? Hegel said that Terror was Kant put into practice. Having started with liberty, virtue, and Reason, the men of '93 ended with pure authority because they believed they were the bearers of truth, that this truth, once embodied in men and in government, is immediately threatened by the freedom of others who as subjects are *suspect*. The Revolution of '93 is Terror because it is abstract and wished to proceed directly to the enforcement of its principles. In view of this, there are two solutions. One might let the Revolution mature and not let it rest on the decisions of the Committee on Public Safety but on the movement of history: that is the solution Hegel may have had in mind in 1807. It is the one Marx adopted. According to *The German Ideology,* the Revolution reduces to a minimum the Terror which is inevitable in human relations and ultimately supersedes it because it is the historical advent of the great mass of men and of a proletariat that is in itself a "universal class." The later Hegel, on the contrary, kept this designation for the officials of an authoritarian state who survey history's meaning for everyone else and create humanity through force and war. In a word, Hegel institutionalizes Terror. He renounces the hypocritical universalism of '93 and since Reason, after all, once it is in power, becomes violence, puts his trust in violence alone to unite men. Today the question is whether the later Hegel is more right than the young Marx.

One cannot postpone indefinitely the need to decide whether or not history has received the proletarian philosophy of history. The world in which we live is ambiguous on this question. But although two, three, or four grains of sand do not make a heap, after a while the heap is there and that nobody can doubt. There is no definite moment that can be pointed to when the compromises cease to be Marxist and become opportunistic. The formulas of *Left-Wing Communism—An Infantile Disorder* embrace almost any possibility. Nevertheless there comes a time when a detour ceases to be a detour, when the dialectic is no longer a dialectic and we enter a new order of history which has nothing in common with Marx's philosophy of the proletariat. It is well known how much Trotsky was attached to this philosophy, to the point of deducing his tactics directly from it without sufficient regard for such outstanding facts as the existence of fascism or the U.S.S.R. For him what continued was *true history,* even if only in the state of a "molecular process" beneath the diversions, the confusions, and the compromises of *everyday history.* However, in his later years he admitted that in the long run this distinction could not be maintained, that if the proletarian philosophy of history is true it ought in the end to shape the events of history, and he finally *set a date for the historical test of Marxism.* "The second world war had begun. Without any question it proved that society could no longer live on the basis of capitalism. Thus the proletariat was subjected to a new and perhaps decisive test." If the war provoked a proletarian revolution, the world and the U.S.S.R. would return to the classical Marxist perspective. On the other hand, if the proletariat does not "take into its own hands the direction of society," the world might evolve in the direction of a monopolistic and authoritarian capitalism. "As onerous as the second perspective is, if the world proletariat proves itself in fact incapable of fulfilling the mission conferred upon it by the course of historical development, nothing else remains than to recognize frankly that the socialist program founded on the internal contradictions of capitalist society has *ended as a utopia.*"[1]

If Trotsky were alive today, could he simply stick to his critique of present history in terms of the proletarian schema? For a long time the proletarian platform enabled him (if not from the objective standpoint of world struggle, at least in his own eyes) to take an independent position equally distant from the fanatics and the counterrevolution-

[1] *The New International,* November 1939, quoted by Dwight Macdonald, *Politics,* April 1946, pp. 97–98.

aries. At the time when he was killed, the moment was perhaps approaching when history would have driven him from this position. All the same he would not have agreed to capitulate before the course of events, nor to join either with monopolistic capitalism or the U.S.S.R. His last writings reveal that in opposition to both tendencies he tried to define a "minimum program" for the defense of the masses. But either this program would have been a variant of "humanistic socialism" and thus have played its role in the world conspiracy against the U.S.S.R., or else (what is most likely) Trotsky would have tried to base it on the movement of the masses and would have come into conflict with the Communist Party. In turn, he himself would have been cornered or confronted with a dilemma. Since history had sundered what Marxism had joined together—the idea of humanism and collective production—either he would have had to opt for an abstract humanism and thus against the only country that had until then established a collective economy, or else he would have sided for a collective economy and the country which stood for it. Either the U.S.S.R. or counterrevolution. One can hardly imagine a "last plea" from Trotsky. To challenge the present or appeal to the future would have been impossible for him since he regarded current experience as crucial. It is unlikely that he would have rallied to the government of the U.S.S.R., for he was, especially in his later years, too much a classical Marxist, too attached to the rationality of the world to live with contradictions and play the romantic game of capitulations and the unhappy consciousness. Political life would have become *impossible* for him.

Here it will doubtless be said that, in effect, there is no political standpoint for those who remain Marxists in the classical sense. But why should we grant a reprieve to this philosophy? It has not succeeded in establishing itself in the facts; it is a utopia. Why consider it any further? This leads us to the last point which it is important for us to establish. The decline of proletarian humanism is not a crucial experience which invalidates the whole of Marxism. It is still valid as a critique of the present world and alternative humanisms. In this respect, at least, *it cannot be surpassed*. Even if it is incapable of shaping world history, it remains powerful enough to discredit other solutions. On close consideration, Marxism is not just any hypothesis that might be replaced tomorrow by some other. It is the simple statement of those conditions without which there would be neither any humanism, in the sense of a mutual relation between men, nor any rationality in history. In this sense Marxism is not a philosophy of history; it is *the* philosophy of history and to renounce it is to dig the grave of Reason in history. After that there remain only dreams or adventures.

A philosophy of history presupposes that human history is not simply a sum of facts side by side—individual decisions and events, ideas, interests, institutions—but that there is in the present and in the flow of events a totality moving toward a privileged state which gives the whole its meaning. Thus there would be no philosophy of history if certain categories of historical facts are insignificant—if, for example, history were made out of the projects of great men. History has a meaning only if there is a logic of human coexistence which does not make any event impossible, but at least through a kind of natural selection eliminates in the long run those events which diverge from the permanent needs of men. Thus any philosophy of history will postulate something like what is called historical materialism—namely, the idea that morals, concepts of law and reality, modes of production and work, are internally related and clarify each other. In a genuine philosophy of history all human activities form a system in which at any moment no problem is separable from the rest, in which economic and other problems are part of a larger problem, where, finally, the productive forces of the economy are of cultural significance just as, inversely, ideologies are of economic significance.

Very well, you may say, but the Marxist conception of history claims even more. It claims that economic history will only achieve stability through the collective appropriation of nature at the hands of the proletariat. From this standpoint it is the proletariat which receives an historical mission and the focus is on its struggle. Surely this is just one hypothesis among others. Could one not imagine other philosophies of history which would bind men's destiny to the wisdom of the Prince, or of the elders, or to the knowledge of scholars and intellectuals, or of saints, or finally to a system of "checks and balances" in the economic and political order such as characterizes the middle phase of capitalism? But a group of men cannot assume an historical mission—the task of bringing history to an end and creating humanity—unless they are capable of recognizing other men as such and being recognized in turn. Now in the case of the Prince, elders, sages, government officials, or even saints, their historical role consists entirely in controlling others, whether by force or persuasion. And if civilization is defined by a wise balance of power, then the latter civilization is still struggle, violence, and the lack of reciprocity. It is possible to deny that the proletariat will ever be in a position to fulfill its historical mission, or that the condition of the proletariat as described by Marx is sufficient to set a proletarian revolution on the path to a concrete humanism. One may doubt that all history's violence stems from the capitalist system. But it is difficult to deny that as long as the proletariat remains a proletariat, humanity, or the recognition of man by man, remains a dream or a mystification. Marxism perhaps does not have the power to convince us that one day, and in the way it expects, man will be the supreme being for man, but it still makes us understand that humanity is humanity only in name as long as most of mankind lives by selling itself, while some are masters and others slaves.

To say that history is (among other things) the history of ownership and that wherever there is a proletariat there is no humanity is not to advance an hypothesis which would then have to be proved the way one proves a law of physics. It is simply to enunciate a conception of man as a being who is situated in relation to nature and to other men—a view which Hegel develops in his master-slave dialectic adopted by Marx. Do the slaves, once they dispossess the masters, manage to transcend the alternatives of lordship and bondage? That is another question. But, even if this were not to be the outcome, it would not mean that the Marxist philosophy of history should be replaced by some other. It would mean that there is no history—if history means the advent of humanity and humanity the mutual recognition of men as men—and consequently that there is no philosophy of history. It would mean in the end, as Barrès has said, that the world and our existence are a senseless tumult. Perhaps no proletariat will arise to play the historical role accorded to the proletariat in the Marxist system. Perhaps a universal class will never emerge, *but it is clear that no other class can replace the proletariat in this task.* Outside of Marxism there is only the power of the few and the resignation of the rest. The reasons why one hangs on to Marxism and does not easily break with it whatever the "vicissitudes of experience," are now clear; when placed in the perspective of this unique philosophy of history, the "wisdom of history" appears as a series of defeats. Marxism has the first claim, an entirely subjective right to a reprieve inasmuch as it is the only humanism which dares to develop its own consequences.

But from this very fact a second claim arises which is an objective one. Because the proletariat has not achieved power anywhere in the world, it is concluded that events have disproved Marxism, or that "no one is still a Marxist today." This line of reasoning presupposes that Marxism is a closed book and since it has not been institutionalized has nothing more to teach us. It involves overlooking a number of facts which show it to be still alive at least in the background if not the foreground of history. Present-day history is not led by a world proletariat, but from time to time it threatens to make its voice heard again. It is feared by heads of state. But each time it slackens its vigilance, universalism and the hope of social transformation are anesthetized. This is enough for us to regard the Marxist attitude as still attractive, not only as moral criticism but also as an historical hypothesis. Historical materialism is confirmed rather than disproved by the evolution of the U.S.S.R. because there one sees the emergence of a strict hierarchy together with patriotic and religious compromise.

Though it may be true that many things are explicable in terms of the rivalry between the U.S.S.R. and the United States, it should be noted that in the less important countries this rivalry makes use of and is used by the class struggle— the two phenomena forming an ambiguous whole in which one or other element dominates on occasion. Sympathies for the U.S.S.R. and for the United States are distributed predictably enough along the line of class cleavage. We have seen how the British government rallied the masses in a national effort during the war by schemes that were socialistic in nature and were abandoned as soon as the danger passed, as though it were aware of the Marxist law of history that class consciousness weakens patriotism. We saw the Vichy and Madrid governments, at a time when the Communist Party was illegal and hunted down, denounce "internal communism" as more dangerous than the victories of the Red Army, thereby recognizing the class struggle as a spontaneous fact in spite of everything they had done to mystify class consciousness. Undoubtedly, they were interested in proving to the Anglo-Saxons that they were a bulwark against the proletariat. One of them at any rate did not do so badly. Hitler's declarations on the dangers of a European Trotskyism belong to the same kind of propaganda. But like all propaganda this appeal under the pressure of its own problems expresses in an ambiguous language one aspect of the situation, namely, the permanent possibility in every country of a proletarian movement. It would be a mistake to give less importance to the proletariat and the class struggle as political factors than do its most resolute adversaries around the world. We have seen how General de Gaulle, who at first called down a great wave of revolution upon his country, turned away from violence once he set foot in France in order to return to power a group of discredited politicians, and quite confidently decide military, economic, and judiciary problems without any popular intervention. He tempered, discouraged, and exhausted his followers as if the only problem that existed for him was to set the masses back into that state of passivity which is the joy of governments, as if all change necessarily involved revolution which is precisely what Marxists claim.[2]

The behavior of the French proletariat during the German Occupation is another one of those facts which Marxism clarifies and is thus confirmed. It can be said of the industrial proletariat—as a whole and in particular—that even when it worked for or traded with the occupying forces, it remained remarkably insensitive to their propaganda, just as in other contexts it resisted chauvinism. Even the least political elements resisted them—not, of course, with acts of heroism, but with a deep, irresistible force. "All

[2] It will be remarked that General de Gaulle's concern was not the proletariat but the Communist Party of the U.S.S.R. That is probably true, but in aiming at the one he struck the other. All the distinctions in the world cannot disguise the fact that, to the extent it became anti-Communist, de Gaulle's government curtailed freedom, tried to tamper with the electorate and adopted a reactionary stance.

this is none of our affair. This European socialism is not our kind of socialism." As if the proletarian condition were the bearer of an implicit and definitive refusal of reactionary ideas, even when disguised, and possessed of a spontaneous wisdom in complete accordance with Marx's description!

When one considers contemporary history, not statistically and in broad terms but at the level of the individuals who live it, Marxist themes reappear which were considered outworn. In physics nowadays there is no crucial experiment upon which a theory might be declared true or false, but rather a decline of less encompassing theories which progressively cover less of the known facts. This is all the more true in history, where man himself is the most important factor, not nature. As a consequence a theory does not cease to count as an historical factor (and in this sense to be true) until men no longer adhere to it. That a Frenchman, despite the "vicissitudes of experience," should remain a Marxist in principle, is, if you wish, merely a psychological fact. But multiplied by millions this "error" becomes a perfectly objective sociological fact which must express something of the reality of French history. Even when the Communist Party suffers compromises, by reason of its social composition, it alone is capable of defending the farmers against the landowners and it is very difficult to persuade the peasants that they are mistaken to vote for it. Likewise, the homeland of the Revolution ought to live up to the image the masses have of it and introduce into the countries it controls the reforms for which they have waited for a century. In order to explain the fidelity of the urban and industrial proletariat in the face of an objectionable politics of compromise it is

not necessary to resort, as Koestler does, to psychopathology.
The proletariat stays in the Party because it is in it, and as
long as the proletariat is in it, the Communist Party remains
the proletarian party. The allegiance tends to continue of
itself. An anti-Communist claims that a proletarian policy
means the Russians. The answer is, yes, but "the Russians"
means a minimum of the proletarian policy not found elsewhere, at least so long as the proletariat does not try to break
with the U.S.S.R. This is the ambiguous situation that confronts us, where a virulent anti-Communism is a conservative force, even though the Communists have suspended or
abandoned revolutionary politics of the classical type.

Many former Communists close their eyes to this residual
or permanent truth of Marxism and consequently adopt philosophical or political stances which fall short of it rather
than transcend it. They have cut themselves off from a party
which to its followers is not just another party or mutual aid
society, designed for strictly limited purposes, but the seat
of all their hopes and the guarantee of human destiny. To
break with the Party is like breaking with a person; it is an
all or nothing affair. It does not leave the memory of what
preceded untouched. Former Communists are often less fair
to Marxism than those who have never been adherents because for them it is part of the past that was painful to reject
and which they would like to forget altogether. If they did
not grasp the full significance of Marxism while they were
Communists, they can hardly be expected to look at it again
and raise questions about something they have rejected as
totally as one rejects a friend or lover. Perhaps they are hang-
ing on to the inadequate image they had constructed because

it provided a reason for the break. A man who has separated from a woman with whom he once lived can never believe it when she becomes dear to someone else. He knew her better than anyone else from their daily life and the quite different picture that someone else has of her now can only be an illusion. He knows her, the rest are fooled. There is nothing frivolous about such comparisons between politics and personal life. Our relations to ideas are inevitably and with good reason relations to people. That is why, on certain questions, former Communists lack lucidity for a long time.

Koestler's example proves this. To hear him speak of "Marxist scholasticism" and "philosophical jargon"[3] it may be presumed that he never gave any serious thought to the philosophical development, which from the post-Kantians to Marx leads up to the vision of the historical existence of the spirit. As it is, he starts from what he calls the "philosophy of the Commissar," namely, the whole regarded as an assemblage of simple elements: life as a modality of physical nature, man as a modality of life, consciousness as a product or even an appearance—an homogeneous world, stretched out flat without foreground or background; human action explained casually like any physical process; ethics and politics reduced to a utilitarian calculus; in a word, the total affirmation of the "external." Then he discovers freedom in the Cartesian sense as the indubitable experience of my own existence,[4] or consciousness as the first truth. He rejoices in observing everything in modern physics or psychology which

3 *The Yogi and the Commissar,* passim.
4 *Ibid.,* p. 229.

contradicts the philosophy of the Commissar—the discontinuity of quanta, the statistical nature of physical laws, the purely macroscopic validity of determination,[5] and the consequent limitation of "explicative" thought and rehabilitation of value judgment.[6] One can understand that after breathing in the suffocating philosophy of the Commissar he is happy to get away from it. What is less understandable is that he blames Marxism for this and rejects Marxism with the rest. For after all, Koestler could have learned from Hegel and Marx (who is the "realization" of Hegel) that quality is irreducible to quantity, that the whole is irreducible to its parts in virtue of its own law of intrinsic organization, and that there is an *a priori* or inner structure of life and history of which empirical events are the unfolding and of which, in the last analysis, man is the agency.

He would have done better not to have exchanged one naïveté for another, not to have adopted scientism instead of the oceanic feeling. Admittedly, he did not fall into religion. He laughs at those who discover an argument for divine inspiration[7] in the behavior of the electron, or a free will in the living cell comparable to human freedom, or in the limits of exact science generally a proof for the Immaculate Conception.[8] What he wants to oppose to the philosophy of the external world or the philosophy of the Commissar is not the philosophy of the Yogi or the philosophy of the inner life. He rejects them both. The Yogi is wrong to

5 *Ibid.,* p. 235.
6 *Ibid.,* p. 249, 252–253.
7 *Ibid.,* p. 235.
8 *Ibid.,* p. 236.

neglect hygiene and antiseptics.[9] He allows violence to occur and does nothing.[10] "Thus to imply that the only alternative to mechanism is the Church of England, and that the only approach to what we can't touch and see is through Christian dogma, is indeed disarmingly naive. . . ."[11] What he is looking for is a "synthesis"[12] between the philosophy of the external which reduces everything to the framework of causal explanation, and the philosophy of the inward which confines itself to descriptions of the different levels of being and loses sight of their effective relations.[13] "The basic paradox of man's condition, the conflict between freedom and determinism, ethics and logics, or in whatever symbols we like to express it, can only be resolved if, while thinking and acting on the horizontal plane of our existence, we yet remain constantly aware of the vertical dimension. To attain this awareness without losing the other is perhaps the most necessary and most difficult task that our race ever faced."[14]

This is very well expressed. But in practice Koestler inclines toward the Yogi without even avoiding lapses into fanaticism which in the Yogi, as he himself shows, alternate with the inward life.[15] One senses he is tempted, not by religion, which has a feeling for the problems of the world, but by religiosity and escapism. "The age of enlightenment has destroyed faith in personal survival, the scars of this

9 *Ibid.*, p. 10.
10 *Ibid.*, p. 254.
11 *Ibid.*
12 *Ibid.*, p. 255.
13 *Ibid.*, p. 252.
14 *Ibid.*, p. 254.
15 *Ibid.*

operation have never healed. There is a void in every living soul, a deep thirst in all of us."[16] He attributes to Christianity, and so apparently to transcendental beliefs, the idea of a hierarchy of being in which the higher is not explained by the lower,[17] which is rather exaggerated if one thinks of Aristotle. He declares coolly that for three hundred years science has usurped the place of that "other" mode of knowledge, which is extreme if one remembers Descartes' *Meditations,* Kant, and Hegel. He calls this "other" mode of knowledge contemplation and declares that it "survives only in the East and to learn it we have to turn to the East."[18] One is tempted, once again, to refer him to Hegel who explains the Orient so well as the dream of a natural infinite without any historical mediation and held in the motionlessness of death.

We seem to be dealing with a philosophy in retreat: Koestler withdraws from world, leaves his youth behind him and keeps almost nothing of it. When, for example, he speaks of Freud, he does not try to separate the Freudian contribution from its now outdated theoretical framework or from the scientistic prejudices that Freud shared with his generation. He seeks only to preserve a pure domain of values beyond all corporeal and historical influences. The smile of the *Mona Lisa,* must be removed from any association with Leonardo's youth,[19] just as courage and sacrifice must be kept apart from masochism and the "death instinct."[20] Koestler should have looked even in masochism

16 *Ibid.,* p. 226.
17 *Ibid.,* p. 245.
18 *Ibid.,* p. 255.
19 *Ibid.,* p. 247.
20 *Ibid.,* p. 250.

and the death instinct or in infantile conflicts for the first
signs and sketch of the human drama which will be brought
to its fullest expression in the actions and deeds of the adult
who can never be abstracted from them. He should have
brought values and the spirit down to the alleged "biologi-
cal" facts. But instead he claims a separate metaphysical
realm for them, thus cutting himself off from any psychological analysis and criticism of man and handing us over to
the mystifications of our good conscience. Koestler discredits
history and psychology, instead of preserving all the psychological and historical factors in a work or a life and
simply integrating them in a total situation which is offered
to the individual as the theme of his whole life—in which he
is free, moreover, to act in a number of ways, since man
reads into the facts of his life whatever he likes to find there.
Whereas Koestler should have recognized the human significance of the libido as an indeterminate power, capable of
becoming "fixated" and "integrated," if necessary against
Freud's declared principles (though in the spirit of his case
studies), he prudishly demands that love of the other person
be set above somatic conflicts.[21]

Because he has believed for too long in a life without

---

21 He offers the work of de Sade (p. 250) as a good example of an ethic
subjected to "biology," whereas to all appearances de Sade proves rather that on
the human level biology like sociology is charged with a will for the absolute.
In Kirilov's remark in *The Possessed* (p. 248), "When he believes he does not
believe that he believes, and when he does not believe, he does not believe that
he does not believe," Koestler finds no echo of Descartes' evil genius, the expression of an ever possible doubt about the authenticity of our claims and decisions—to be overcome, as Descartes teaches, through the experience of thought
in act. No, for Koestler we must forget the doubt, forget psychology and history,
by postulating once for all that we transcend them.

values and without spirit—and still does—now he can only integrate them again on a higher level. One need only watch Koestler dismiss "dialectic"[22] and reinstate allegedly clear thinking in the name of the "elementary laws of logic," of which some contemporary examples of "ready-made beliefs,"[23] "thalamic"[24] reasoning, and schizoid mentality are offered as a terrifying counterproof. He imagines it is possible to overcome the contradictions in life by suppressing one of the two terms which constitute them, as if the dialectic was responsible for its own abuse and the cause did not lie in the increasing contradictions experienced by humanity, and as if the rules of thought could stop at the simplest ideas, because they are the clearest, even at the risk of failing to understand events. In the same way, Koestler wages a war on the formula "To understand all is to forgive all" and pulverizes it with that abstract logic whose secret he shares with the supporters of *Polemic*. In effect, what he is saying is that either I understand an action in itself, and if it is bad this understanding can only lead me to condemn it more severely, or else to understand an action is to explain it in terms of external causes such as environment, heredity, or circumstances, and then I am treating action as a simple natural product which would not affect my judgment of it as a free action. But what if our actions were neither necessary in the sense of natural necessity nor free in the sense of a decision *ex nihilo*? In particular, what if in the social order no one were innocent and no one absolutely guilty?

22 *Ibid.*, p. 237, n.1.
23 *Ibid.*, p. 122.
24 *Ibid.*, p. 132.

What if it were the very essence of history to impute to us responsibilities which are never entirely ours? What if all freedom is a decision in a situation which is not chosen but assumed all the same? We would then be in the painful situation of never being able to condemn with good conscience, although it is inevitable that we exercise condemnation.

This is what Koestler does not want. For fear of having to forgive, he prefers not to understand. We have had enough of ambiguities, he thinks, enough of problems and puzzles. Let us get back to absolute values and clear ideas. Perhaps in his case it is a matter of health and one is reluctant to interfere with a cure. But then he should not offer a remedy for his own uncertainty as a solution for the problem of our times. He burns the philosophy of the Commissar, which he once adored. This does not inspire much confidence in his present statements. Koestler's essays exhibit a "round-trip" style similar to that of many former Communists—but annoying to others. After all, we do not have to atone for the sins of Koestler's youth; and if, at the age of twenty he was disposed toward "the rationalism, the superficial optimism, the ruthless logic, the arrogant self-assurance, the Promethean attitude of the nineteenth century,"[25] that is no reason for destroying with these attitudes the contribution of the nineteenth century, and now leaning toward "mysticism, romanticism, the irrational ethical values, . . . medieval twilight." Nor is it any reason to offer the masses, who can make nothing of it and meanwhile continue their sacrificial existence, an "anti-materialist nostalgia" which is

[25] *Ibid.*, p. 19.

as vain as materialism itself. We have no love for these bright, new truths. As Montaigne says, "Just between us, I have always observed a remarkable accord between super-celestial opinions and subterranean morals."[26] A certain ostentatious cult of values, of moral purity, of the inward man is secretly akin to violence, hate, and fanaticism. Koestler knows this, for he warns us against the "Mystic who acts as an inverted Commissar."[27] We like a man who changes because he is maturing and understands more today than he did yesterday. But a man who reverts to his old stand is not changing, he does not go beyond his errors.

It is in the area of politics that Koestler's humanism shows its vicious side. Here, as elsewhere, he does not progress; he breaks with his past, in other words, he remains the same. In only one passage of his book is there any mention of the type of Marxist revolutionary produced by the nineteenth century which falls between the types of the Commissar and the Yogi. "Since Rosa Luxemburg there has arisen no man or woman endowed with both the oceanic feeling and the momentum of action."[28] This leads us to understand that neither Rosa Luxemburg nor, we may add, any of the great Marxists of this century have professed, or at any rate lived, the sordid philosophy of the Commissar. Thus if today's communism has departed from its original inspiration, then it should so be said, but *in no case does the remedy lie in reverting to the game of the entirely inward life* whose mystifications have been exposed once for all by Marxism.

---

[26] *Essays,* III, XIII.
[27] *The Yogi and the Commissar,* p. 254.
[28] *Ibid.,* p. 16.

Koestler forgets what he should have kept from his Communist past—the sense of the concrete—and keeps what he should have forgotten—the disjunction between the inward and the external. He is both too faithful and not faithful enough to his past, like those patients of Freud who remain fixated to their experiences and for this reason are unable to understand, embrace, and eliminate them.

Koestler calmly praises British "socialism": "The constitutional framework of British democracy provides at least a chance for a relatively smooth transition to Socialism. . . ."[29] "He adds that one of the basic teachings of Marxism is the importance for the proletariat of preserving certain democratic liberties in the state."[30] The fact that socialism and British democracy rest upon the exploitation of a part of the world is passed over. What is more, Koestler is aware that English socialists have been relieved of any scruples they might have had left, and that such conscientious proletarians as are left have lost whatever universalism they had. "That famous sentence in the *Communist Manifesto:* 'The workers have no fatherland' is inhuman and untrue. The farm-labourer, miner or roadsweeper is bound to his native village or street, to the traditions of language and habit, by emotional ties as strong as those of the rich. To go against these ties is to go against human nature—as doctrinaire Socialism with its materialist roots so often did."[31]

If a proletariat ever emerges from provincialism and chauvinism, Koestler can be relied upon to drive it back. It is

[29] *Ibid.,* p. 225.
[30] *Ibid.,* p. 224.
[31] *Ibid.,* p. 219.

difficult to understand why, in a recent interview, his sole reproach against the Labour Party was that it had not created an International (without asking himself what the reasons might be for this regrettable omission). After the famine of Karkov we can understand that Koestler appreciates the moral climate of beautiful and melancholy England. Naturally, no one likes restrictions or the police. No one with any feeling has ever doubted that it is more agreeable to live in those countries which, thanks to their historical advancement and their natural resources (supplemented by the revenues of a usurious government), assure their citizens a standard of living and liberty which a developing collective economy has to deny its people. *But that is not the question.* Even if tomorrow the United States become the master of the world, it is clear enough that neither its prosperity nor its constitution would thereby spread universally. Even if France had aligned herself politically with the United States, she would not for all that have known the relative prosperity that Belgium, for example, owes to its possession of the Congo. She would have had to pay for United States imports whose production costs are the highest in the world. In the same manner, we must appreciate Russian problems and solutions in terms of the Russian standpoint. Koestler's manner of speaking about the Karkov famine and electricity failures is reminiscent of certain French journalists before the war who talked of rationing, bread lines, and poverty in the U.S.S.R. Since then we have experienced the same thing, and for nothing. Some of the American soldiers faced with the spectacle of our sordid life did not show any compassion, but a kind of contempt and shock, probably imagining that no one who has not sinned greatly can be so miserable. Something analogous happened to certain of our compatriots who sojourned to the United States during the Occupation. By the same token, among many continentals there is a kind of sympathy for those people who go hungry and have experienced need.

It is not by an appeal to feelings that we shall resolve the question which, once again, is not to know whether things are better here or there, but whether (and which) one of the systems is endowed with an historical mission. We raised the question in relation to the U.S.S.R. It must also be raised with regard to British socialism. We must ask whether a "Socialism" which abandons internationalism, at least "in its doctrinaire form," and accepts without scruple the outcome of Churchill's foreign policy is of any interest to men in the rest of the world, and whether socialism understood in this sense is not just another name for imperialist politics. The French voters, according to the anti-Communist, in voting for Marxism are playing the Russians' game. But how is it that he does not see that "humanistic socialism" is precisely the mark that Western imperialism should wear in order to be recognized as an historical enterprise? It is amazing to see Koestler so sensitive to the first equivocation, yet so insensitive to the second. He appeals to "Western revolutionary humanism."[32] But in other respects he has no criticism of the internal policies of the Labour Party whose revolutionary spirit has been known for what it is for sometime. As to his humanism, he hopes for peace; but the whole question is to know how he means to achieve it and, as they

32 *Ibid.*, p. 225.

say in school, by what *means* we should proceed toward that honorable *end*. In this regard, *The Yogi and the Commissar* demonstrates very well that anti-Communism and humanism possess two ethics: one which they profess, celestial and uncompromising, and one which they practice, terrestrial and even subterranean.

How convincingly the Left Communists proved during the days of Munich that appeasement leads not to peace but to war —and how thoroughly they have forgotten the sermons which they preached! In the case of Russia as in that of Germany, appeasement is based on the logical fallacy that an expanding power, if left alone, will automatically reach a state of saturation. But history proves the contrary. A yielding environment acts as a vacuum, a constant incentive to further expansion, and gives the aggressor no indication how far he can go without risking a major conflict; it is a direct invitation to him to overplay his hand and stumble into war by sheer miscalculations. Both world wars actually arose from such miscalculations. Appeasement transforms the field of international politics from a chessboard into a poker table: in the first case both partners knew where they are, in the second they don't. Thus the opposite of appeasement is not bellicosity, but a clearly outlined, firmly principled policy which leaves the partner in no doubt how far he can go. It does not eliminate the possibility of war but prevents the danger of stumbling blindly into it; and that is as much as political wisdom can achieve. It is highly unlikely that any great power will commit an act of aggression against a small nation if it is clearly and definitely understood by all concerned that a new world war will be the inevitable consequence.[33]

[33] *Ibid.*, p. 221–222.

This is the conclusion of so many scrupulous meditations on the problem of means and ends. In the last sentences the whole thing is blessed with *si vis pacem*. Alas! If the pacifism of the leftist journalists today reminds Koestler of the policy of appeasement in the years 1938 and 1939, he too, with his *si vis pacem* reminds us of something. In 1939 there were two ways of taking the world lightly. One was to say in effect that Germany could be disarmed by making concessions; the other was to say that Germany was bluffing and that war could be avoided by toughness. We were taught in 1939 that appeasement leads to war but also that toughness is hardly serious unless it is implicitly a consent to war, perhaps even a desire for war. For consent, being conditional, is merely caprice, and the antagonist, once he knows this, acts accordingly. The tough powers may devote themselves entirely to war preparations, in which case their threats carry force—but no matter how peaceful their ends, the adversary overlooks them and draws his conclusion from the tanks, artillery, and fleet he sees. Or the powers may forswear belligerent means and then diplomatic firmness becomes ineffectual. Are we to conclude then that from today on, England and the United States should prepare for war in the same way they did for the invasion of 1940 to 1944? Is it to be assumed henceforth that the U.S.S.R. cannot coexist with the rest of the world? That is the real question, for it is impossible to present the threat of a world war as a means of assuring peace when we have seen Germany in 1941 carry the war into the East without having crushed the West. Nor is it possible to appeal to a united front among the powers to isolate the aggressor, for he is never without accomplices, the variety of interests among the powers being too great for all to side against the aggressor.

True firmness demands that one take the state of war for granted. This is indeed a political standpoint, but not one that can be called "humanist" without abusing language. Moreover, it is still to be feared that here too the means may devour the ends. Once the United States has crushed the U.S.S.R., Koestler (if he survives) has only to offer the people of Western Europe (if any remain) a new policy of "firmness" toward the United States as an "expanding power." It is easy to imagine a new essay of Koestler's, perhaps entitled, *Anatomy of a Myth* or *The End of an Illusion,* this time dedicated to the Anglo-Saxon countries. In a short space he could show that the United States, with its anti-Semitism, racism, and strikebreaking, is only nominally the "land of the free," and that the remaining "ideological bases" of Labour Party socialism are inadequate for the justification of the British Empire's foreign policy. Perhaps after this double detour by way of shameful means, the Yogi could finally proceed directly toward humanist goals.

Koestler will object that we are criticizing him with the language of radical pacificism which today belongs to the Soviet fifth column, just as in 1939 it belonged to the Nazi fifth column. But it is not we who proclaim abstract humanism, the purity of means, and the oceanic feeling. It is he—and it is his own argument that we are turning on him. We are showing that if one applies Koestler's principles without compromise, they condemn Anglo-Saxon and Soviet politics alike and make it impossible to define a political position in the world as it is, and that if, on the other hand, one seeks to spread his principles over the world by force, employing the power of the British as a support and banner, we would be brought back with these same principles into the play of eternal history which would transform them into their opposites.

Communism cannot be justified simply by showing that violence is a component of Western humanism as an historical force, since it still has to be known whether Communist violence is, as Marx thought, "progressive." Far less does violence provide communism with that spineless assent which pacificism, whether it means to or not, historically gives to violent regimes. But this means depriving Western politics of that wonderfully clear conscience which is so remarkable in much of contemporary Anglo-Saxon· writing. It puts the debate between the Western democracies and communism into its proper domain, which is not a debate between the Yogi and the Commissar but between one Commissar and another. If the events of the last thirty years lead us to doubt that the world proletariat is about to unite, or that proletarian power in one country establishes reciprocal relations among men, they in no way affect the truth of that other Marxist idea that no matter how real and precious the humanism of capitalist societies may be for those who enjoy it, it does not filter down to the common man and does not eliminate unemployment, war, or colonial exploitation. Consequently, when set against the history of all men, like the freedom of the ancient city, it is the privilege of the few and not the property of the many. How do we answer an Indochinese or an Arab who reminds us that he has seen a lot of our arms but not much of our humanism? Who dares to say

that, after all, humanity has always progressed in the hands
of a few and been sustained by its delegates and that we are
that elite and the rest have only to wait their turn? Yet this
would be the only honest reply. But this would mean
acknowledging that Western humanism is a *humanism of
comprehension*—a few mount guard around the treasure of
Western culture; the rest are subservient. It would mean that
Western humanism, like the Hegelian State, subordinates
empirical humanity to a certain idea of man and its supporting institutions. It would imply that in the end Western
Humanism has nothing in common with a *humanism in
extension,* which acknowledges in every man a power more
precious than his productive capacity, not in virtue of being
an organism endowed with such and such a talent, but as a
being capable of self-determination and of situating himself
in the world.

In its own eyes Western humanism appears as the love of
humanity, but for the rest of men it is only the custom and
institution of a group of men, their password and occasionally their battle cry. The British Empire did not send Yogi
missions into Indonesia, any more than the French in Indochina, to teach "change from within." Their intervention
in these countries has involved, to say the least, a "change
from without" and a rough one. If the reply is that their
forces are defending freedom and civilization, this implies
a renunciation of absolute morality and entitles the Communists to say that their forces are defending an economic system which will put an end to man's exploitation of man. It
is from the conservative West that communism received the
notion of history and learned to relativize moral judgment.

It has not forgotten the lesson and has sought, at least in a given historical milieu, those forces which on balance have a chance of making humanity a reality. If one does not believe that the proletariat can acquire power or that it can deliver what Marxism expects of it, then perhaps those capitalist civilizations which despite their imperfections have at least the merit of existing represent the least of history's horrors. But then the differences between them and the Soviet enterprise is not the difference between heaven and hell or between good and evil; it is only a matter of the different uses of violence. Communism should be thought about and discussed as an attempt to solve the human problem and not be treated as an occasion for heated argument. It is a definite merit of Marxism and an advance in Western thought to have learned to confront ideas with the social functions they claim to articulate, to compare our perspective with others, and to relate our ethics to our politics. Any defense of the West which forgets these truths is a mystification.

Conclusion

AT FIRST MARXISM was the idea that history has two poles—
at one end is audacity, the élan of the future and the will to
create humanity, and at the other end is prudence, the
weight of the past, the spirit of conservation, and respect for
the "eternal laws" of society; and these two directions select
and reinforce whatever adds to them. On a local scale this
can be verified any day. But Marxism is also the idea that
these two outlooks are transmitted historically by two classes.
In the older countries the outlook of the capitalist sectors is
largely what can be expected from a Marxist schema. However, it seems that American capitalism possesses such natural
resources and is in an historical situation which for a time
enables it to monopolize the spirit of audacity and enterprise.
The world proletariat, on the other hand, to the extent that
it is directed by the Communist Party, is oriented toward tactical wisdom, or where it is free from it, is too exhausted
or divided by the diversion of world wars to exercise its
radically critical function. Thus the leading roles in history
are held by agents in whom it is difficult to recognize the

classical descriptions of "capitalism" and the "proletariat" and whose historical activity remains ambiguous. A Frenchman, an Italian, or a Spanish republican would soon say that the political question put in terms of a rivalry between the United States and the U.S.S.R. is "poorly posed." A war between these two powers would create the greatest confusion, and whether a holy crusade was ever possible, now is not the time. The two powers would undoubtedly find the certitudes they need in their own patriotism. But the middling powers could not share in these attitudes. There is no future in it for them and there will be no light in history except through peace. The middling powers do not count for much and their intellectuals count even less. *Our role is perhaps not very important. But we should not abandon it.* Whether it is effective or not, our task is to clarify the ideological situation, to underline, beyond the paradoxes and contingencies of contemporary history, the true terms of the human problem, to recall Marxists to their humanist inspiration, to remind the democracies of their fundamental hypocrisy, and to keep intact against propaganda the chances that might still be left for history to become enlightened once again.

If we were to try to draw up out of this at least a provisional political strategy, the principal rules would be the following:—

1. Any critique of communism or the U.S.S.R. which makes use of isolated facts without situating them in their context and in relation to the problems of the U.S.S.R., or any apology for democratic regimes which is silent about their violent intervention in the rest of the world, or juggles

the records to make it appear a special case—in short, any policy which does not seek to "understand" these rival societies in their totality can only serve to mask the problem of capitalism, to threaten the very existence of the U.S.S.R., and should be regarded as an act of war.

Within the U.S.S.R. violence and deception have official status while humanity is to be found in daily life. On the contrary, in democracies the principles are humane but deception and violence rule daily life. On top of that, propaganda has a fine game. Comparisons only make sense between wholes taking into account their circumstances. It is useless to confront a fragment of Soviet history with our practices and laws. An enterprise such as that of the U.S.S.R., which began and was pursued in the midst of general hostility, in a country with immense resources but which has never known the level of culture and standard of living of the West, and, finally, which more than any other of the Allies has borne the brunt of war, cannot be judged in terms of facts taken out of context. The treatment of Dreyfus on Devil's Isle, the suicide of Colonel Henry (who was left his razor) and that of one of his collaborators, also a forger (who was left his shoelaces), are perhaps more shameful in a country favored by history than the execution of Bukharin or the deportation of a family in the U.S.S.R. It would certainly be quite false to imagine every Soviet citizen subject to the same supervision and exposed to the same dangers as the intellectuals and the military—as false as to imagine the fate of the accused before French justice in terms of the Dreyfus Affair. The death sentence of Socrates and the Dreyfus Affair left intact the fame of Athens and

France for "humanism." There are no reasons for applying different criteria to the U.S.S.R. The Soviet government has just increased the mobilization of youth labor. In Europe, where the S.T.O.[1] is still remembered, it is easy to make a propaganda attack out of this. But what can the U.S.S.R. do when it has lost seven million men and is reconstructing without any appreciable aid? Do they want her to have taken all her manpower out of Germany? If she had to satisfy all the critics, there would be nothing left for her but to abandon the game and to abdicate her independence. This sort of criticism is aimed at the very existence of the regime.

2. Our second rule might be that humanism excludes a preventive war against the U.S.S.R.

Here we are not thinking of the pacifist argument that war is as bad as the evils it pretends to avoid. We accept the idea of wars, as at least necessary, if not just. The war against Nazi Germany was such a war because the logic of the system led to the domination of Europe. The case of the U.S.S.R., on the contrary, is not so clear. It may well be that Soviet society purveys reactionary ideologies along with Marxist humanism, makes use of the profit motive as well as socialist motives, and subscribes simultaneously to the equality of labor and the hierarchy of salaries and power. But it is not founded upon a nationalist ideology nor forced to find its economic equilibrium in war production or the conquest of foreign markets. A war against the U.S.S.R. would not only reduce the threat of a great power, it would also destroy the principle of a socialist economy. It is enough to recall the tones in which the Republicans in America spoke of the

[1] Service du Travail Obligatoire. (Translator)

"reds" and "radicals" who had "infiltrated" the Roosevelt
Administration, to imagine the attitude of the French ruling
clique in the event of an American victory over the U.S.S.R.
In order to make war on the U.S.S.R. a French government
would have to begin by silencing a third of the French electorate and representatives and most of the representatives of
the working class. For these reasons, a preventive war against
the U.S.S.R. cannot be "progressive" and would pose for
every "progressive" a problem such that never arose in the
war against Nazi Germany.

3. Our third rule would be to remind ourselves that we
are not in a state of war and that there is no Russian aggression—which is the second difference between the Russian
and the German case. Strategically, the U.S.S.R. and the
Communists are on the defensive. The propagandists want
to make us believe that we are already at war and that therefore it is necessary to be for or against, to go to prison or to
imprison the Communists.

The way Koestler speaks of Russian expansion, one would
really think the U.S.S.R. held Europe in its hand through a
series of seizures comparable to those of Hitler. In reality
"Russian expansion" in Europe began one day at Stalingrad
to end with the war at Prague and on the frontiers of Yugoslavia. At that time no one raised any objections. What has
changed since then? Is it that the Russians have not set up
free elections everywhere? But what can be said for the
Greek elections? Or that the Russians have deported families from Poland and the Baltic States? But there are 15,000
Jews in Bergen-Belsen while British troops are guarding the
Palestine frontier. Moreover, neither Roosevelt nor Churchill

were children. They knew well enough that the U.S.S.R. was not fighting in order to restore everywhere parliamentary rule and liberties. We always forget the clauses in the secret agreements signed by Roosevelt, though if the Republicans in America threaten the Democrats with their publication, it can hardly be doubted that they would reveal a rather rash Roosevelt. What has changed since 1945 is the state of mind of the Anglo-American governments, and one is obliged to restate that the U.S.S.R. ceded over the Azerbaidjan, Trieste, and Yugoslav incidents.

All the same, have the Communists in France changed so much since 1944? A French writer, who has since strongly fought against tripartism and the Communist Party said to me, thinking at the time of reconstruction: "One thing is sure, we cannot do anything without them." What has happened since then? They have not seriously tried to rule alone with the Socialists as they could have done, and whenever their electoral successes push them into the foreground they announce a rather cautious offensive, as they did at the vote on the first Constitution. Yet, when the voters do not follow them, they withdraw without struggle to the stand on the union of Frenchmen. And lastly, they always looked for the remedy for tripartism much less in a fighting government than in an enlarged government. Here as well they are to be found on the defensive and perhaps all they want in France are firm guarantees against a military coalition. In sum, in the accusations brought by the Anglo-Americans against the U.S.S.R. and the Communists one finds hardly any new facts since 1945. The whole question at bottom is to know whether they have really accepted the fact of a Soviet victory (itself made possible by the delays on the Second Front), or whether they are now trying to avoid the quite foreseeable consequences of that victory. As things stand, one cannot speak of Soviet aggression.[2]

All right, then, the U.S.S.R. is on the defensive. But that is because she is weak. Tomorrow, if she were in a position of strength, she would terrorize Europe. The Communist parties would drop their democratic habits and imprison everyone who did not think correctly, including those naive people who presently are its defenders abroad. Every plea on behalf of a weak U.S.S.R. made today becomes an act of complicity with an aggressive Russia tomorrow. The critics, even the sympathetic ones, have no effect on communism, whereas what one says in favor of it serves it just as it is. One is either for Communism or against it. For a long time to come, at least, there can be no third position. This is a strong argument and the risk does exist. It seems to us that it is necessary to run the risk. We hold that the war has not started, that the choice is not between war with the U.S.S.R. or submission to it; that the life of the U.S.S.R. is not incompatible with the independence of Western countries; that in the nature of events there is still a minimum of free play enough to speak of truth and to oppose propaganda with something else than counterpropaganda; and that one cannot hide the truths that are verifiable today in the name of the possible truths of tomorrow. If it happens tomorrow that the U.S.S.R. threatens to invade Europe and to set up in every country

[2] Germany and Italy were able to send whole divisions into Spain without provoking Anglo-American intervention. Indirect and intermittent aid from Yugoslavia and Bulgaria to the Greek partisans is enough for them to proclaim that liberty is endangered.

a government of its choice, a different question would arise and would have to be examined. That question does not arise at the moment. What we are urging against anti-Communism is not the famous "it is always good to enjoy an hour's peace." It is simply the truth upon which we believe we still have a hold despite all the propaganda. If history is irrational, then it has periods in which intellectuals are not tolerable and enlightenment is forbidden. While they have the platform one cannot ask them to say anything other than what they see. Their golden rule is that human life and history in particular are compatible with truth *provided only that all its aspects are clarified*. This is perhaps a foolhardy opinion but it is one which must be held. It is, so to speak, man's professional risk. Any other behavior is an anticipation of war, falls into American propaganda in trying to avoid Russian propaganda, and throws itself immediately into myths for fear of falling into them later.[3]

This sort of conclusion is upsetting. To speak of humanism without being on the side of "humanist socialism" in the Anglo-American way, to "understand" the Communists without being a Communist, is to set oneself very high—in any case, way above the crowd. Actually it represents noth-

---

[3] These remarks would only apply to internal politics if the parties openly admitted the Communists' presence in the government and if the Communists then effectively followed their general line of agreement with the "formal" democracies. In France they are not creating a proletarian revolution and yet they keep up the Bolshevik political forms which are obviously incompatible with the working of "formal" democracy. A choice has to be made between Bolshevism and the pluralist principle of the Popular Front. The coexistence of the Communist Party and other parties will remain difficult as long as it does not elaborate and put into practice the theory of a "Western Communism" implicit in Thorez's recent statements to the Anglo-American press. C.f. Preface, p. xxv below.

ing more than a refusal to commit oneself to confusion removed from truth. Is it our fault that Western humanism is warped because it is also a war machine? And what if the Marxist enterprise has only been able to survive by changing its nature? When people demand a "solution," they imply that the world and human coexistence are comparable to a geometry problem in which there is an unknown but not an indeterminate factor and where what one is looking for is related to the data and their possible relationships in terms of a rule. But the question that we face today is precisely that of knowing whether humanity is simply a *problem* of that sort. We are well aware of what it involves, namely, the recognition of man by man—but also that, until now, men have only recognized one another implicitly, in conflict and the race for power. The constants in the human problem indeed form a system, but a system of conflicts. The question is to know whether they can be overcome.

Hegel said: "The maxim: 'Ignore the consequences of actions' and the other: 'Judge actions by their consequences and make these the criterion of right and good' are both alike maxims of the abstract Understanding."[4] He rejected realism as well as moralism because he had in mind a stage of history where good intentions would no longer bear poisoned fruits, in which the rules of action were identical with those of conscience, because he believed in a Reason beyond the alternatives of interior and exterior which enables man to lead simultaneously a conscious and an empirical life—to be the same for himself as he is for others. Marx

---

[4] *Philosophy of Right.* Translated with Notes by T. M. Knox, Oxford, Clarendon Press, 1942; paragraph 118, p. 80.

was less positive, since he suspended this synthesis in favor of human initiative and more resolutely withdrew from it any metaphysical guarantee. Contemporary philosophers have not renounced rationality or the harmony of the self with itself and with the other person, but only the pretense of a reason content to be right for itself and removed from the judgment of the other person.

It does not show much love for reason to define it in such a way that it is the privilege of a Western elite released of all responsibility toward the rest of the world and in particular of the duty to understand the variety of historical situations. To seek harmony with ourselves and others, in a word, truth, not only in *a priori* reflection and solitary thought but through the experience of concrete situations and in a living dialogue with others apart from which internal evidence cannot validate its universal right, is the exact contrary of irrationalism, since it accepts our incoherence and conflict with others as constants but assumes we are able to minimize them. It rules out the inevitability of reason as well as that of chaos. It is not that it is in favor of the conflict of opinions so much as it assumes such conflict from the very start. How could it do otherwise? One is not an "existentialist" for no reason at all, and there is as much "existentialism"—in the sense of paradox, division, anxiety, and decision—in the *Report of the Court Proceedings* at Moscow as in the works of Heidegger. Existentialist philosophy, they say, is the expression of a dislocated world. Indeed, and that is what constitutes its truth.

The whole question is to know whether if we take our conflicts and divisions seriously it cripples or cures us. Hegel often speaks of a *bad identity,* meaning an abstract identity which has not integrated the differences and will not survive their manifestation. In an analogous way, one could speak of a *bad existentialism,* which exhausts itself in the description of the collision between reason and the contradictions of experience and terminates in the consciousness of defeat. But that is nothing but a renewal of classical skepticism—and an incomplete description. For the very moment we assert that unity and reason do not *exist* and that opinions are carried along by discordant options which remain below the level of reason, the consciousness that we gain of the irrationalism and contingency in us cancels them as fatalities and opens us to the other person. Doubt and disagreement are facts, but so is the strange pretension we all have of thinking the truth, our capacity for taking the other's position to judge ourselves, our need to have our opinions recognized by him and to justify our choices before him—in short the experience of the other person as an *alter ego* in the very course of discussion. *The human world is an open or unfinished system and the same radical contingency which threatens it with discord also rescues it from the inevitability of disorder and prevents us from despairing of it,* providing only that one remembers its various machineries are actually men and tries to maintain and expand man's relations to man.

Such a philosophy cannot tell us *that* humanity will be realized as though it possessed some knowledge apart and were not itself embarked upon experience, being only a more acute consciousness of it. But it awakens us to the importance of daily events and action. For it is a philosophy which arouses in us a love for our times which are not the simple repetition of human eternity nor merely the conclusion to premises already postulated. It is a view which like the most fragile object of perception—a soap bubble, or a wave—or like the most simple dialogue, embraces indivisibly all the order and all the disorder of the world.